THE ALEX

The Story of The Alexandra Hotel, Bridlington

Martin Wallace

The Alex © Martin Wallace 2019

First published 2019

Second edition 2020

Revised 2022

ISBN 978-0-244-16822-3

The right of Martin Wallace to be identified as the author of this work has been asserted by him in accordance with the Copyright, Design and Patents Act 1988.

25 South Back Lane
Bridlington
www.lodgebooks.co.uk

Other titles by the author

Movin' On: The Story of the Area of St Mark's Forest Gate
(Pub: St Marks, Forest Gate PCC. 1986)

Healing Encounters in the City (Pub: Grove Books. 1987)

City Prayers (Pub: Canterbury Press. 1994)

The Celtic Connection (Pub: Aquila Celtic Crafts. 1995)

Celtic Reflections (Pub: Tim Tiley Publishing. 1995)

Pocket Celtic Prayers (Pub: Church House Publishing. 1996)

Celtic Heroes of Faith (Pub: Aquila Celtic Crafts. 1996)

Practical Celtic Spirituality (Pub: Aquila Celtic Crafts. 1997)

The Celtic Resource Book (Pub: Church House Publishing. 1998)

Worship, Window of the Urban Church (contrib)
(Pub: SPCK. 2006)

In Good Company: A History of the Village of Barton Le Street
(Pub: Barton le Street PCC. 2008)

CONTENTS

INTRODUCTION   1

(i) RIGHT PLACE, RIGHT TIME

1. WIDE OPEN SPACES   7

2. A CHILD OF HER TIME   9

3. THE CONTEXT – A TIMELINE   15

4. INVENTING THE SEASIDE   19

5. SLEEPING BY THE SEA   29

(ii) IMAGINATION, FLAIR AND STYLE

6. THE ALEX IS BORN   33

7. WHAT'S IN A NAME?   41

8. A HYDRO HOTEL   47

9. APPEARANCES ARE EVERYTHING   53

10. ARE THERE ANY DETECTIVES OUT THERE?   83

11. MORE THAN JUST A GARDEN   87

12. THE SEA VERSUS THE LAND   95

(iii) HIGH DRAMA

13. LIFEBOATS AND BATHING HUTS   103

14. PLANS FOR EXPANSION – AND A MANICURE!   111

15. THE 1924 SALE   115

16. TOO WELL CONNECTED? 121

17. A ROYAL SCANDAL 125

18. A LESS RISKY GUEST 127

19. OTHER DISTINGUISHED GUESTS, REAL AND IMAGINERY 129

20. THE ACID BATH MURDERER 135

(iv) TEAMS AND DREAMS

21. BELOW STAIRS 185

22. THE HATJE DYNASTY 195

23. JOLLY HARD WORK! 199

24. THE TIFFANY YEARS 211

25. TWO DIFFERENT CAREERS SET IN MOTION? 221

26. THE FINAL CURTAIN 227

(v) A GENEROUS LEGACY

27. THANKS FOR THE MEMORY 239

28. THE SPIRIT OF THE ALEX LIVES ON! 249

BIBLIOGRAPHY 295

ACKNOWLEDGEMENTS 298

INTRODUCTION

For over a hundred years the grand Alexandra Hotel stood proudly on the seafront at Bridlington gazing out to the horizon. During these years thousands of guests signed the Visitors' Book, and hundreds of staff drew their weekly wages. For a century, the walls witnessed and quietly absorbed the antics of those who walked its corridors, slept in its bedrooms, ate in its dining room, drank in its bar, danced in its ballroom, agonised over the accounts and worked in its kitchen.

Hotels are places we visit in order to do those things we would not normally do at home. This might be something as innocuous as having the time to read a book curled up by a roaring fire, or simply enjoying having good food served with no threat of dirty dishes to wash afterwards. Alternatively, they can be places to engage in risky behaviour away from the usual circle of friends, family and neighbours. For hotel proprietors they can be places to test dreams about being adventurous entrepreneurs, and proving to surprised parents and teachers that you could be successful after all.

So, at The Alexandra Hotel what business deals were agreed in the gentlemen's smoking room? How many lovers met in the garden after dark away from the watchful eye of parents or guardians? Which proposals of marriage were accepted in the corridors at the end of the evening? How many lasting friendships were kindled in the lounge? What happened when the Yorkshire Puddings collapsed in the kitchen? Who panicked when the lift stalled? Who owned up when the bath overflowed? Whose longed-for baby was conceived on the second floor? How much was gambled on a game of billiards? Before the age of computers, how often did the ballroom act as a dating site, offering the chance to cuddle a partner with absolutely no commitment?

These and countless other questions will remain forever unanswered, probably to the relief of some of those involved. When the hotel breathed its last and was demolished, amongst the rubble were buried forever many of the stories that would fascinate us. There are inevitably many secrets that will remain forever hidden, and questions that will remain unanswered.

However, with a little detective work there are other riddles we can solve. Who invested a huge sum of money and why was the hotel built in the first place? Why was that particular site on Bridlington's North Beach chosen? What made the 1860s the right time to build? Why was it called the "Alexandra"? Who decided on the chosen style of architecture? Why were the front gardens so large? Why did one of the wealthiest shipping magnates stay there? What was the connection with the Prince of Wales' appearance in court? What attracted famous authors and politicians to stay there? Did anyone realise one of the guests would later be called a "vampire" by the national press? Was it a total coincidence that a fire gutted the upper floor just as it was being sold in the final auction?

What follows, therefore, is not always a simple chronological account of names and dates, but rather a thematic approach to peeling back the layers, and having fun as we look beneath the surface. It is about making connections and seeing links that could be easy to miss. The early chapters set the scene and then, having done that, we can begin to meet some of the wonderfully colourful characters who step across the stage.

So let's have some fun playing detective with both the details and the broader picture. What unfolds is a fascinating insight into how seaside resorts, and Bridlington in particular, both reflected and contributed to the life of the nation. What is so intriguing is to see how this was all so focussed in the story of the Alexandra Hotel, affectionately known as "The Alex".

And "fun" is the key word here. The Alexandra Hotel stood overlooking the beach – a place of fun. For some this means building sandcastles or playing rounders or just sunbathing. For others it means throwing stones in the sea, paddling in the shallows, splashing in the surf or swimming energetically. Fun on the beach means different things for different people.

So with this book: approach it with a sense of fun and freedom. Some will want to enjoy the pictures. Some will want to dive straight into the chapters about the murderer, the naughty prince or the career paths. Some will want to begin with the more recent memories towards the end of the book. Some will simply start at the beginning and finish at the last page.

It really doesn't matter. Just enjoy the fun of the stories with as much freedom as we enjoy the beach

(i) RIGHT PLACE, RIGHT TIME

1. WIDE OPEN SPACES

No one coming to Bridlington can fail to be impressed by the wide open space that is set before them. The vast bay offers an uninterrupted view of the horizon from the lofty white cliffs of Flamborough Head in the north to the long finger of Spurn Point pointing out to sea in the south, marking the entrance to the busy ports of the Humber. On the broad promenades there is nothing to disturb the great sweep of the sky. The vast sandy beaches are washed clean every day by nature as the tide ebbs and flows across the flat surface. The sea wall makes a clear statement with its straight clear line: mastery of the boundary between the sea and the land is firmly established by determined human engineering.

On North Beach, in front of the Alexandra Hotel were large open landscaped gardens. Nearly four acres of tidy floral grounds offered a tranquil base from which all of this could be enjoyed. For those who lived further inland, whose lives were often hemmed in by buildings, busyness, work, noise and anxiety, space was what they sought, and The Alex offered just that.

The wide open space of the front gardens was an indication of what lay in store inside the hotel: an airy entrance hall, broad corridors with open plan lounges, high windows allowing bright light to stream in, spacious bedrooms, and a vast ballroom and dining hall. The service offered was to be calm and efficient.

The Alexandra Hotel was envisioned as a place where people could come and find space – space and calm to re-connect with everything that is important. Here was a place for people to meet again with their own innermost being, their souls. Here was a place for people to meet in depth with those around. Here was a place for people to meet with nature. Here was a place for people to meet with their purpose in life, and return home with a clearer mind, a bolder spring in their step, and a more joyful song in their heart.

This is the story of how one hotel, in one town, took on that challenge, and how its legacy lives on today.

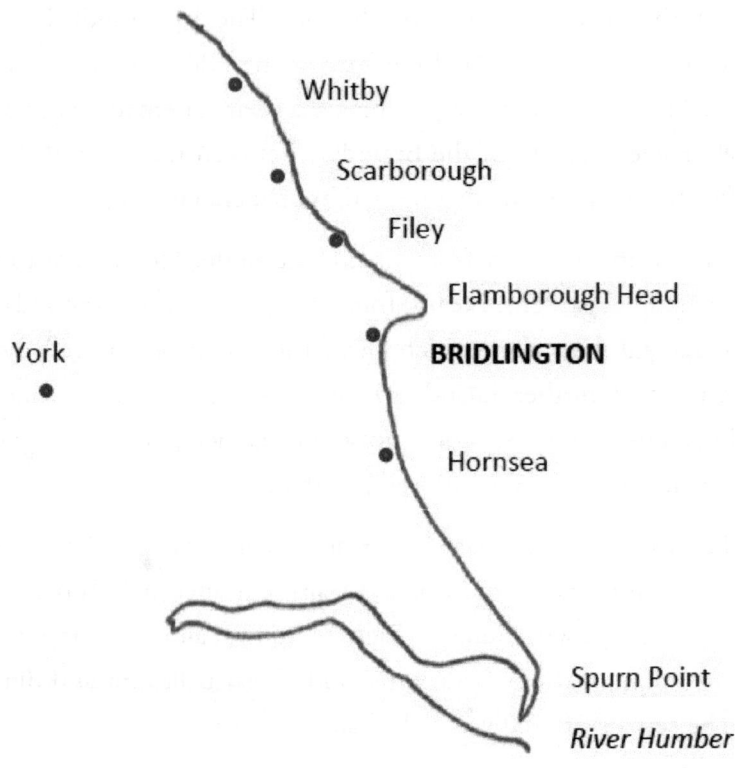

Bridlington and its neighbouring resorts on the Yorkshire coast.

2. A CHILD OF HER TIME

It is strange but true that organisations and buildings behave in many ways just like we do, as individual human beings. They are affected by what goes on around and within them, and respond just like we do – sometimes sympathetically and sometimes obstinately. The imposing, majestic Alexandra Hotel, which once dominated the North Beach of Bridlington, is no exception.

None of us lives in a vacuum, and we can only understand our own lives when we take note of the times in which we live. In the same way, the Alexandra Hotel, its conception, birth, infancy, adolescence, adult life, and eventual years of decline – all these are the result, and a reflection, of great forces both beyond and within its walls.

It was conceived and born in an era of unparalleled growth, confidence, discovery, invention and optimism. Britain had exploited its trade routes across the world and secured a hold on vast tracts of land in other continents. It controlled and protected its shipping lanes, bought raw materials at very low prices, and sold manufactured goods for a huge profit. Shipping magnates, tradespeople, industrialists and the military all appear as our story unfolds.

The farming revolution had introduced new machinery into the fields of the countryside and, combined with better understanding of animal husbandry, produced more and better food for the growing population – and some of this food was served in the hotel by maids and waiters whose families had once tilled the soil of the farms of Yorkshire and beyond.

The industrial revolution created huge factories in the towns and cities with the result that different materials were now available for building a new hotel and upholstering its soft furnishing, and in time those who worked in these towns came to stay as guests, dance in its ballroom, and take tea in its ornate gardens.

An ever-growing network of railways, roads, inland waterways and ocean-going ships all transported both goods and people to the hotel at a high speed and at a low cost not imaginable a few decades earlier.

Cutting-edge technology pioneered by imaginative engineers ushered in a whole new world: clean water was piped direct to homes, flushing toilets brought new standards of cleanliness, underground sewers took human waste far away, gas extended the hours of daylight and made heated rooms and cooking easier to perfect, new gadgets for the kitchen and for cleaning the rooms made life seem suddenly much more bright, hygienic, controlled and efficient. The level of service hotels could offer was revolutionised, and they sprung up all around the coast – including at The Alex.

The town of Bridlington itself is set on the north-eastern edge of the country. Sometimes, this might seem to be a disadvantage economically, because it can feel a long distance from the centres of national activity. But in fact this has its own very distinct advantages. The edge can be an exciting place to visit, as those guests who walked from the hotel along the exposed cliffs to Sewerby would have discovered.

At the edge people can see what others miss as they have to peer across the clutter of "stuff" that gathers further inland. At the edge, quite literally, new horizons are seen. It is at the edge that excitement is experienced that can be had nowhere else. As we walk along a cliff path it is difficult not to feel drawn as close as possible to the edge itself to peer over. We are attracted to danger. We know that one careless step and we will fall. If that happens, we will be able to blame no one else. Here we cannot project blame or guilt elsewhere. We realise we are responsible for ourselves. Our decisions are our own. Body, soul and mind all engage together to experience the excitement but keep us safe. The adrenalin pumps as never before. It is here we see things from a different perspective and big decisions are made about life, love, ambition, work, friendships, family, money, and so on. That is why today the cliff path along Sewerby cliffs is lined with seats. They form the open-air psychiatrist's couch, the therapist's clinic, the vicar's study, the mystic's meditation centre, the counsellor's lounge, the medical consultant's room. They are all there, free for the taking, and offering the chance to come and untangle the affairs of the soul, clarify the mind and refresh the body. It was all on the doorstep of the Alexandra Hotel and we see this in some of the stories.

For others, however, this "edge" provided the possibility of something quite different. For those hiding secrets or seeking clandestine activities, it offered the hope of an escape from the intrusive glare of publicity and investigation. This too we see in the stories of some of those who stayed here.

Yet, despite its location on the edge of the country, Bridlington could not avoid being swept up in this nineteenth century fervour of excitement. Local entrepreneurs grew in confidence and new finance became available. As in all conceptions, lust and love both played their part in the creation of the Alexandra Hotel: a lust for profit and a love of the Yorkshire coast. This was a time when the sea was beginning to beckon people for reasons other than traditional fishing for food, or as a means of transport by boat. The coast with its fresh air, clean salt water, and the playground of the sandy beach all combined to encourage new ideas for those able to exploit and enjoy them.

Those who had accumulated vast wealth were among those who first had the vision for a grand hotel, had the courage to invest their money, had the ability to oversee its construction and then had the confidence to manage it. Their wealthy peers were among the first guests who, as we shall see, brought with them both their gracefulness and their disgracefulness!

But nothing in life is static – "the only thing in life that never changes is change itself!" As the twentieth century unfolded so it brought seismic shifts in the world. In two world wars some nations were destroyed and new ones created. New lines were drawn in international trade and political alliances. As some lost their wealth new fortunes were being made by others. Britain often found it difficult to engage with this new state of affairs. Its colonies demanded independence and threw off the shackles of slavery. They formed the new British Empire which later became the Commonwealth, indicating a more adult relationship with this country. The old class-structure was breaking down both at home, and internationally.

In this climate, it became increasingly difficult for the Alexandra Hotel to maintain its air of superior, genteel, gracious living. As holidaymakers changed in what they wanted, what they could afford, and where they came from, so the hotel no longer stood as the bright new youngster on the coast. Rather, it increasingly seemed to be the grand old lady sinking into gentle decay, gradually breathing more slowly and less deeply, unable to keep up with the demands of the time and competition from elsewhere.

For just over one hundred years, guests had sat inside its windows gazing out over the water. As the sunlight reflected on the waves so they reflected on their lives. They marvelled, year after year, at the great golden globe of the sun as it rose over the watery eastern horizon. They relaxed as they watched the evening clouds turn pastel pink and blue from reflecting the sunset in the west behind the hotel. They trembled as they witnessed the winds and the rain batter the unprotected coast.

Guests had sat in the lounges and debated the merits and faults of a total of six monarchs who had ruled over them, and then nineteen prime ministers in no less than twenty-six governments (some of whom had led the country more than once between 1866 and 1976). Their arrival, once in genteel horse-drawn carriages, and then courtesy of the railway, later was then in coaches, on motorbikes and in cars. Starched collars and crinoline dresses walking by on the promenade gave way to tee-shirts and baseball caps. Silver service by maids in the hotel was supplanted by burgers and pizzas in cardboard boxes in the open air. Formal foxtrots and waltzes were replaced by jazz musicians and the frenzied jitterbug, and then in turn by lively skiffle groups and noisy pop groups, some of whom played and stayed at The Alex in its later years.

None of this evolution and revolution should surprise us, especially at the coast. The seaside is inevitably a place of change. The tides and current constantly alter the local beach sweeping its sand and stones in and out, depositing and then removing seaweed, lobster pots, seashells and timber from submerged forests. The coastline moves with the powerful surge of the mighty waves. It seems inevitable, therefore, that the whole understanding of the seaside will also be in a state of constant flux with its offerings of food and drink, cinemas and theatres, arcades and clubs and churches and parks. It always will be evolving, and if for whatever reason, a hotel cannot also evolve to match this movement, it will eventually breathe its last, as did the Alexandra Hotel.

But within those walls we find there was a treasure chest of humanity – people who laughed and loved, cried and argued, plotted and schemed, made and lost friends, dreamed and wondered – and who all returned home different because of staying there.

Bridlington has for centuries been a place for refreshment and renewal. Thousands of pilgrims came to the shrine of St John of Bridlington at the Priory church to pray and return different. Indeed, Henry the Fifth came to pray there in 1415 before the Battle of Agincourt. He then went into battle, invigorated and strengthened, and was victorious over a French army twice the size of his own. Sailors anchored in this "Bay of Refuge" to find shelter from the treacherous storms of the North Sea. Bridlington has always been a place of generous hospitality. The very words hospital, hospitality, hostel and hotel all share the same root. The Alex played a key role in this ongoing reputation, and this is its story.

3. THE CONTEXT – A TIMELINE

It can be very difficult today to grasp the extraordinary development and changes that formed the context for the life of the Alexandra Hotel. A random trawl through just some of the more dramatic events, however, can give some indication.

1805	Battle of Trafalgar
1806	Bridlington's first lifeboat service established
1811	Bridlington's population 3,741
1813	Gas lighting introduced into London's streets
1815	Napoleon defeated at Waterloo
1829	First railway opened: Stockton to Darlington
1829	London Police Force established
1833	Gas service established in Bridlington (The Burlington Gas Light Company)
1837	Queen Victoria is crowned
	Penny post established
1841	David Livingstone begins to explore Africa
1842	A painting shows the harbour with wooden piers and a gas lamp is shown
1844	Bishops Improved Baths built on Esplanade, near Bridlington harbour
1846	Railway opened from Hull to Bridlington
1848	Revolutions swept across Europe
1851	The Great Exhibition
	The first Singer sewing machine was produced

1854	The Crimean War
1858	The formation of the Londesborough Masonic Lodge
1859	Bridlington Free Press founded
1861-1865	American Civil War
1865	First plans for piped water in Bridlington
1866	**Alexandra Hotel opened**
1867	Princes Parade opened along the seafront
1869	Suez Canal opened
1871	Manchester was producing one third of the world's cotton goods
	Holy Trinity Church in the adjacent road is consecrated
1878	St Anne's Orphanage and Convalescent Home opened in the road next to the hotel.
1879	Alexandra sea wall built
1881	Wyatt Earp won a gunfight at the OK Corral in America's still very Wild West
1882	The outlaw Jesse James shot dead in America's Wild West
1888	Trinity Cut Bridge (The Donkey Bridge) built next to the hotel
1889	Eiffel Tower built in Paris
1891	Bridlington's population 6,840
1890	Bridlington seafront is lit by electricity: seven arc lamps and forty-seven incandescent lamps light Princes Parade and the Victoria Rooms, for the summer season only

1896	Daily donkey rides introduced on the beach
	314,484 visitors arrived in Bridlington by rail, many as day trippers
	First telephone exchange opened in Bridlington
1897	**Alexandra Hotel installs Bridlington's first telephone: Number "1"**
1899	Bridlington Fire Brigade formed
1901	Bridlington's population 12,482
	Queen Victoria died and Edward VII is crowned
1905	Bridlington town is lit by electricity
1907	Floral clock installed
	The Alexandra Hotel is extended
1910	George V crowned
1911	Bridlington's population 14,334
1914-1918	First World War
1920	**Plans to further extend the Alexandra Hotel unveiled**
1923	Nearby Floral Hall destroyed by fire
1931	Completion of North Sea Wall
1932	Spa Royal Hall destroyed by fire
1933	Victoria Rooms destroyed by fire
1936	Sewerby Hall opened by Amy Johnson
	Edward VIII becomes king: George VI crowned
1937	The Expanse Hotel opened on North Beach
1939-1945	Second World War
1940	Woolworth store and Notarianni's Cafe hit by bomb

1941	St Anne's Convalescent Home in the adjacent street hit by parachute land mine
1953	Elizabeth II crowned
1957	Russia's Sputnik enters space
	Elvis Presley's "All Shook Up" is No 1 in the UK Charts
1962	The Mini is launched
1963	The Beatles' "From Me To You" is No 1 in the UK Charts
1965	America enters the Vietnam War
	The direct railway line to York is closed
1972	The railway line to Scarborough is reduced to single track
1973	**Alexandra Hotel – first fire**
1975	**Alexandra Hotel closes, and a fire seals its fate**
1976	**Alexandra Hotel demolished**
1979	Bridlington's population 28,590 – a number which doubles at the height of the summer season

Such a timeline shows the extraordinary era of invention, optimism and change in which the Alexandra Hotel was set, and a selection of the events which would undoubtedly have been at the heart of conversations among both staff and guests, as well as all the more local gossip we all take for granted.

4. INVENTING THE SEASIDE

Today, we take so much of Bridlington for granted – buckets and spades, sandcastles and beach-huts, deckchairs and windbreaks, sea walls and promenades, candy floss and ice cream, fish and chips, hot dogs and fairground rides, cafes and pubs, restaurants and postcards, theatres and cinemas, amusement arcades and gardens – and hotels. But it was obviously not always so. In fact, they are all inventions of the last three hundred years, and all have been developed in order to attract people to this wonderful place we call "the seaside".

For most of human history, people have regarded the sea as at worst a ferocious wild enemy, tempestuous and moody, ready to devour any who dare to risk their lives on it, and at best a means of transport and a breeding ground for the fish we love to eat. Even today, the sea is still treated with respect, a force to be reckoned with which can overturn ocean going liners and huge tankers. Its sudden storms can sweep away whole townships and wreak havoc on local life. In addition to all that, at a very basic level the British people seem to have a natural in-built aversion to entering cold water at all!

In the eighteenth century few people ventured out into the sea to fish, except the very poorest who lived in closest proximity to the harbour, and who often had to combat terrible conditions. Most of these fishermen were never able to work regularly from week to week in their small boats because of the variable weather and the unpredictable availability of fish. The life of the fishermen was both precarious and mysterious.

To those who lived further inland, these people who faced the perils of the sea were seen as a hardy but strange breed of people. They were romanticised in novels but studiously avoided at close quarters. They had a strong fishy smell and a way of life all their own. Tourists were often advised to ensure they outnumbered the local boatmen if ever they ventured into the harbour for a pleasure trip.

Bridlington, set in its sheltered "Bay of Refuge", however, was a port of some significance and early pictures often show a very large number of cargo vessels at anchor. But in time the associated boat-building industry declined and the fishing industry changed. The town and its coast had to find new reasons to exist, just as all communities do when old industries are challenged.

In the eighteenth century the only people who worked regularly were (some of!) the gentry and it was these folk who had the money which enabled them to travel. But they visited inland spas and had servants to bring bowls of tepid water to their bedrooms. The cold open sea as a place to visit for refreshment was in no one's mind until the second half of the century, when George the Fourth, when he was previously Prince Regent, made Brighton on the south coast a fashionable place to visit. But even then, people went to bathe, to have a bath in the sea, not to swim, sunbathe and have fun on the beach – that all came much later. It was all about "taking the waters".

But good fortune smiled on Bridlington. The Duchess of Manchester as early as 1732 had led the way popularising "dipping your body in the sea" at nearby Scarborough, entering the water by means of a horse-drawn shed on wheels. She was following the lead given by physician Dr Richard Russell (1687-1759) who championed sea water as a cure for scurvy, jaundice, gonorrhoea and gout. He recommended mixing half a pint of sea water and drinking it with generous amounts of milk – or port! What is more, where the Spa Theatre now stands, the Chalybeate Springs were discovered, their waters mineralised with iron salts, which could be marketed as very health-giving. This was a double bonus for the town.

With better roads, others were able to follow suit to "take the waters", this time at Bridlington. At first these were the aristocracy, the wealthy merchants and the genteel families who stayed with friends inland and visited for the day. Those recorded as venturing to Bridlington include Lord and Lady Wentworth, the Duke and Duchess of Leeds, the Duke and Duchess of Newcastle, and the Duke of Devonshire. Some began looking for suitable local houses to own, such as Henry Boynton of Burton Agnes and Christopher Sykes of Sledmere.

By 1813 there were sixty-six lodging houses in King Street. In 1839 Charlotte Bronte stayed in number 5 Garrison Square. When the railway came in 1846 it suddenly brought the coast within reach for a much wider group of people. In many ways the coming of the railways was a rude shock to the system, and like a bolt of electricity brought the town of Bridlington alight. Indeed, it is difficult to see how Bridlington could have developed, or The Alex could have been built, without the coming of the railways. Like all coastal settlements, Bridlington is relatively remote and roads were hazardous at the best of times but now the town was being transformed in ways that no one could have foreseen.

Even popular novels were making the point that it was the railways which revolutionised coastal towns. For example, Charles Lutwidge Dodson, better known as Lewis Carroll, was a regular visitor to the seaside. He would have known all about Bridlington as his uncle, Charles Lutwidge, was the vicar of nearby Burton Agnes. His curate was the brother of Ellen Nussey, a very close friend of Charlotte Bronte, and it was he who suggested that Charlotte and Ellen visit Bridlington for a holiday in 1839. When Lewis Carroll later published "Alice's Adventures in Wonderland" in 1865 (just a year before The Alex opened) he wrote: "(Alice's) first idea was that she had somehow fallen into the sea, 'and in that case I can go back by railway,' she said to herself. Alice had been to the seaside once in her life and had come to the general conclusion, that whenever you go on the English coast you find a number of bathing machines in the sea, some children digging in the sand with wooden spades, then a row of lodging houses, and behind them a railway station."

With this steady new influx of people, more lodging houses were needed, and within that at least one grand hotel was seen as economically viable. The Alex in 1866 was the response, and its "chateauesque" style raised the profile of Bridlington above that of most other towns on the east coast.

Nearby, townhouses were built in Marlborough Terrace and The Crescent in 1869-71. Elegance began to prevail on the north side of the harbour. The old fishing village was evolving fast into a spa town and then into a resort. The working harbour was being infiltrated by those who saw it as a playground for the rich, who then in turn had to make way for the new money of the middle-class industrialists, who then themselves found even they had to make way for the newly mobile working classes.

In previous centuries, very few people had the opportunity to have a break from work or consider spending time at the coast. In fact, the whole notion of a holiday had only ever taken hold as the Christian church took a stand against unscrupulous local lords and employers, and designated certain days as saints days, "holy days", decreeing that people must be given time off work to attend church to worship. Together with Christmas, Easter, Whitsunday and Harvest, the number of holy-days (holidays) began to increase, and often the rest of the day could be spent celebrating the festival with friends and family.

But even then it took Christian social reformers like Lord Shaftesbury and others a long time to secure the Acts of Parliament which guaranteed better working conditions for the masses, including holidays of several days together. In the background, however, seeing the potential, entrepreneurs began to build places for people to stay, eat and drink. Seaside villages became towns, and for those hemmed in by living and working in enclosed unhealthy spaces, the seaside began to be realised as a place for the heart and mind to be enlarged. The wide open space of the horizon, uninterrupted by walls, roofs and noise was, and is, highly therapeutic. Those in industrial cities whose surroundings seemed like a filthy, noisy prison, suddenly discovered freedom as children could run around on the sand, play games and make noises which no longer echoed through dingy alleyways. People suddenly had a space to reinvent themselves, to realise that life was bigger and better than the cramped conditions back at home.

A person's soul at last could say to itself: "I am more than just an anonymous cog in an industrial wheel. I am a person. I am of value. In this apparently faceless universe I can relate to what it is really all about. I can appreciate the personality of the flaming sun as it rises over the sea. I can feel the restfulness of the universe as the light rearranges itself on the water in the evening. I can see the clouds riding like chariots in the clear sky. I can relax in the rhythm of the tides as the sea flows in and out. From before I was here, and long after I have gone, the sea will always follow the pull of the moon. I understand that although my own existence may be full of constraints and turmoil, life itself is much more than that. The universe has a purpose and a direction, and within that so does my own life. God is in His heaven and all is well."

Few, of course, will have put it quite like that, but that will have been the effect. What is more, it will have been the same for both the factory workers and those better off. The more leisured classes could, of course, often stay for a considerable time at a hotel such as The Alex. On the other hand, the working classes might only come for the day or at most a week, staying in a cramped boarding house as holidays carried no pay. It was not until 1871 that the first Bank Holiday Act guaranteed Easter Monday, Boxing Day, Whitsunday and a day's holiday in August for all workers, and it was not until 1932 that the Holidays With Pay Act guaranteed one week of leave with pay. But in the overall scheme of things, it was the combination of the upper, middle and working classes who all contributed to the local economy, re-creating Bridlington from a fishing port into also a seaside resort.

All those who came, from all classes, were "holidaymakers" – and the phrase is no coincidence. Holidays were, and are, "made" by the people who invest, innovate, build and work in a place. The environment is created, and then the people come to play, laugh, have fun, make new friends, and enjoy the beaches and the buildings. It is the visitors and the guests who "make" the holidays. They are not just passive recipients, for without them the resort would be nothing more than a ghost town. Not just consumers, they are the creators of its life, and their stories are therefore the attraction of the place – what they get up to, how they form new friendships, and how they return restored and refreshed.

Strangely, until about 1750 most of the population worked in the open air in the fields or on roads and buildings. But when the industrial revolution took hold, even the middle classes began to spend most of their time indoors in offices, factories and at home. The sun-tanned complexions of earlier times gave way to pale skin which became championed as a sign of beauty, especially for women.

We had to wait until the 1920s for sunshine to be appreciated as a health-giving option. It was recognised more widely that people who spent all year in industrial cities, rarely seeing the sun through the haze of smoke, breathing sulphurous fumes, and surrounded by noisy machinery, could really be nourished by time at the seaside. People realised that holidays at the coast made people healthier, brighter, more full of vitamins, and, in fact, better neighbours, better parents and better workers. The beach became a place to play and sunbathe. The front garden at the Alexandra Hotel became an oasis in which to take tea, sit in the sun, and even ride around its perimeter paths on a hired donkey.

But this was a double-edged sword. In time it was the love of sunshine itself which encouraged the rise of cheaper package holidays abroad as wages rose after the Second World War. Mediterranean countries like Spain offered dependable sunshine throughout a much longer summer in a way that Bridlington could not match.

Travel was also having its impact. It was the new invention of the railways that had brought the masses to Bridlington along its set tracks. The early charabancs and coaches which used to park in huge numbers behind the hotel performed the same service. They had hard wooden seats and were open to the elements or had a heavy canvas hood which could be swung over the passengers. They were not comfortable but they were exciting as they offered the chance of a brief stay at the seaside.

But then in the 1930s, the popularity of the motor car meant people could choose their own destinations, and not necessarily follow the chosen routes of the railway or coach company. Then again in the 1960s the development of package holidays with economy airlines meant overseas travel began to be within the reach of more and more people. In the early days the bracing east winds may have been an important component in advertising the town as a place to come to revive ailing health, but by the second half of the twentieth century people's preferences had become much more focussed on sunbeds in Spain.

Trouble for the hotel trade was being heralded. Large establishments like The Alex had to adapt to a clientele with less money, those who could not afford to travel abroad. Lower charges meant less income, and that meant less money available for maintenance and repairs. The very thing that had encouraged the hotel to be built, the invention of the seaside holiday, had also brought buried deep within it the very seeds of its own demise.

Bridlington, placed among a selection of British seaside resorts.

5. SLEEPING BY THE SEA

The mixture of accommodation we see today in seaside resorts evolved very gradually and at varying speeds. The first visitors to "take the waters" at Bridlington would often only stay for the day, being accommodated by friends or family further inland. But as the attraction of the seaside grew, so providing local accommodation was seen as a way to earn an income.

Occasional rooms were rented out, and slowly the number of boarding houses and lodgings increased. These often had very few amenities and overcrowding was normal. Those with money began to take rooms in larger houses and in time whole houses were rented, not just for the week but for the "summer season". Parents, children, maids and butlers all came and needed proper accommodation. Private developers built crescents and terraces specifically for this market.

Small, private hotels could accommodate a few families and offer some comfort, but were often of dubious quality and had petty restrictions about access, noise and food. It was around 1850 that the grand hotels like The Alex began to appear for the wealthy, who would stay for anything from a few days to a whole season.

These hotels were often built in a style variously described as chateauesque, French, or neo-Gothic, and deliberately copied the style of those in the fashionable resorts of the French and Italian Riviera. They were large scale enterprises, expensive to build, but with good commercial potential because they provided high-end accommodation. Flattering descriptions abounded in guide books: "resplendent", "monumental", "iconic", "sumptuous", "exclusive".

Visually dominant, in significant sites and with unparalleled sea views, they offered all the spaces, rooms and services that could be desired, but they were very definitely for the select few. Town Councils, however, would be more than happy with this. Wealthy guests brought valuable revenue to the town which in turn raised opportunities for employment. The high price of accommodation would deter the undesirables, just as surely as did the uniformed hotel doorman and the strict codes of dress and behaviour to be observed in their public rooms. Indeed, the working classes in general would have felt quite daunted by the expansive gardens, grand lobbies and wide doors and corridors. The Alex stood as a proud participant in this great new seaside movement, a showpiece for the town determined now to be successful and socially aspiring.

(ii) IMAGINATION, FLAIR AND STYLE

6. THE ALEX IS BORN

The year that changed everything for Bridlington was 1846, the year the railway line from Hull was opened. But the effect was not immediate. In that year the town could offer one hundred and thirty-four boarding and lodging houses and sixteen inns and taverns. Five years later in 1851 the number was still exactly the same, and even as late as 1867 the newly arrived editor of the Bridlington Free Press said he found "things as lethargic as could be". But new life was stirring.

In 1864 the first houses in Sewerby Terrace were completed, the terrace in which the Alexandra Hotel would be built. Indeed, in 1865 one of the houses in Sewerby Terrace is described as "a residence for genteel families and comprises on the ground floor a dining and breakfast room; four bedrooms; on the second floor seven bedrooms; in the attic seven good rooms; in the basement a housekeeper's room, a bedroom, a kitchen, a scullery and pantries; and the owners for a small fee have the privilege of entrance to the small pleasure ground in the front of three acres sloping down to the sea beach." This was clearly a very smart road in which to locate a new hotel.

It was in 1864 that a number of shareholders registered the "Bridlington Quay Alexandra Hotel Company Limited", helped by the recent Stock Companies Act of 1844 which enabled private enterprise to raise capital and flourish. These men were Mr Prickett, Mr Hutchinson, Mr Mann, Mr Beauvais, Mr R. N. Beauvais (his brother), Mr B. S. Saunders (a brick-maker), and Mr W. B. Stewart (a Scarborough architect). The company acquired the necessary land with the help of some of the townsmen and the architect was commissioned – no less than shareholder W. B. Stewart. Perhaps Mr Saunders as a brick-maker was also involved in the actual construction?

William Baldwin Stewart was a notable local architect. He was responsible for three particularly significant buildings in Scarborough. He had designed Westborough Methodist Church in 1862 which still stands as a Grade II Listed Building, and is reckoned to be his finest work. Three years later in 1865 he designed the gateway to the old prison in Dean Road and Castle Road, and when the prison was closed the gateway continued in use as a store and depot by the Town Council. After he saw the Alexandra Hotel completed, he designed Scarborough Town Hall (1869-70), originally as a private residence for the Woodall family. This Jacobean-style mansion with Dutch gables and leaded domes and turrets is also now a Grade II Listed Building.

In 1863, The Bridlington Quay Gazette reported that on 17th October the directors had agreed to "proceed immediately with the building of a large and elegant hotel offering uninterrupted and splendid views of The German Ocean and the beautiful cliffs of Flamborough. A good family hotel has long been called for…" That same day the architect lost no time and advertised in newspapers inviting tenders from building firms.

The Alexandra Hotel was built between 1864 and 1866. In April 1864 a serious accident briefly stopped work when some of the arches forming the landings of the main staircase gave way. Crashing through four storeys came brickwork and cement, together with the foreman William Trott, and two joiners, John Archer and John Wilson, who were all buried in the rubble and seriously injured. Nothing further is known about their final condition beyond this report in the Leeds Mercury of 4th April 1864, but work clearly continued to proceed swiftly – perhaps a comment on the value placed on the lives of working men in those days?

Mr Barr, the hotel's builder (who had also built houses in Sewerby Terrace), claimed that when completed it was "one of the most beautiful of modern structures to be found in any of the sea-bathing places of the east coast, and Scarborough has nothing comparable with it."

An advert in a York newspaper demonstrates the confidence the shareholders had in their project. An entry in the York Gazette dated 3rd December 1864 reads: "The Alexandra Hotel. To be let, from the 6th day of April next, this newly erected Family Hotel, situated on the North Cliff in Bridlington Quay, with an uninterrupted view of the German Ocean, and the beautiful cliffs at Flamborough. Further details may be obtained on application to J. Stephenson, Secretary to the Alexandra Hotel Company Bridlington, 19th November 1864."

The hotel finally opened with a celebration dinner on Wednesday 13th July 1866. It was a grand affair. The Hull Advertiser and Exchange Gazette of 14th July 1866 recorded: "the dinner was held in the dining hall of the hotel. The dinner was attended by a large number of influential gentlemen of the district, besides visitors from Hull, Leeds and other towns. The company included the Reverend

Canon Hey, The Reverends H. F. Barnes and J. Blanchard, Dr King (Hull), Dr Hutchinson (Bridlington), Dr Spark (Leeds), Captain Makins (1st Yorkshire Volunteers), R D Preston Esq. (Midland Circuit), Messrs T. W. Palmer, W. R. Richardson (Richardson and Sons), H. Wilson, J. Fearne, Mr Finningley (Hull) etc. The hotel is the most elegant and commodious in Bridlington Quay, and occupies a site unsurpassed by any on the Yorkshire Coast. The hotel commands a beautiful and extensive view of the picturesque bay of Bridlington, with the white cliffs extending to Flamborough Head; and on the south pier, the new sea wall and promenade now being constructed. The hotel contains about seventy rooms, comprising a large dining room, drawing room, sitting rooms etc., and the whole having been furnished in a good and substantial manner by Messrs Richardson and Sons, Bond Street, Hull. It is now completely full of visitors, and is occupied by Mr Edwin Taylor, who has so successfully conducted The Crescent Hotel at Filey, and until recently the George Hotel, Hull."

The hotel also had a "coffee room for gentlemen", a billiard room, and a smoke room. Board and lodging rates in that first year were six shillings and sixpence per day for a "public room" and seven shillings and sixpence per day for a "private room". Children under twelve were charged half price and servants were accommodated at four shillings per day. By the end of 1866 the hotel's seventy guests included the Barkwith family from Cottingham Castle near Hull, and Consul Huniman and his party from Stockholm.

Once it was completed, the attention of the hotel's shareholders and their friends turned to the adjacent land. To the south was a seven-acre field known as Beacons Field (so named because a beacon had stood there since the sixteenth century). This field was owned by Captain Charles and Miss Lucy Makins. They had built a sea wall along the eastern perimeter of the estate, and sold the field to Mr R. N. Beauvais (one of the hotel's shareholders), Thomas Harland and Robert Raiston Brown who between them developed the Beaconsfield Estate, consisting of Beaconsfield Crescent and the neighbouring roads.

Mr R. N. Beauvais (1817-96) was a retired sea captain, born at Ulrome, and had been a churchwarden at the Priory for twenty-seven years. He was also, as a very wealthy man, one of the principal contributors to the cost of the Priory's restoration. Thomas Harland was also a churchwarden at the Priory and another generous benefactor to the restoration appeal. He was a leading figure in the town, an Assistant Lord Feoffee from 1861 and a Lord Feoffee from 1878 together with being a Harbour Commissioner. Both Beauvais and Harland were staunch and public supporters of the Conservative Party. Robert Brown (1818-1898) is more of a mystery. He described himself in the 1871 Census as an "annuitant", someone who lives on a provided annuity (an allowance or a sum from a will), and who was simply born "at sea".

The block of land either side of Carr Lane (now Sands Lane) was put up for sale in sixty-two building plots the same year as the hotel was opened, 1866.

By 1871, Captain Edward Barnes was living in the grand house overlooking the sea, on the north side next to the hotel, called Danes Lea (now demolished), and he later sold it to Thomas Harland who lived there with his wife, daughter, governess, lady's maid, cook, two housemaids, a kitchen maid and a butler. It was Captain Barnes who founded the St Anne's Orphanage and Convalescent Home in 1878 in St Anne's Road next to the hotel, including the controversial "iron church" within it, which the Archbishop of York tried unsuccessfully to prevent being used for Anglo-Catholic worship.

Meanwhile, the original investors were all no doubt working hard behind the scenes to ensure the success of their new project, The Alexandra Hotel. Mr Prickett, one of the wealthy shareholders, who in 1864 initially registered the company which built the hotel, also owned The Avenue Hall in Westgate, Old Town. This large, imposing house which had been built for his family around 1714, later became The Avenue Hospital, a maternity hospital serving the town, and is now residential apartments.

Like all his fellow shareholders, Mr Prickett was a very busy man locally. In 1868, just two years after the hotel opened, he was elected President of The Bridlington Cricket Club. Then ten years later in 1878, as the club sought to establish itself on a firmer footing, the Bridlington Free Press reported that "a meeting was held at The Alexandra Tap on Monday (18th May) for the purpose of forming a cricket club for Bridlington Quay…It was resolved that a club be formed to be called The Bridlington Quay Cricket Club."

The intriguing little fact tucked into that report is the reference to meeting at "The Alexandra Tap". What and where was this? The club's normal practice had been to hold its meetings at The Crown in Quay Road, so why the change of venue? A "tap *bar*" was the usual description given to a bar which sold draught beer "on tap", direct from the tap of a barrel. A "tap *room*" was where local craft beers could be sampled, often with food served and meetings held.

So where was this Alexandra Tap? It was clearly not a room in the hotel itself, but probably an establishment very close by and therefore well known to Mr Pricket. On 29th September 1889 the local court received an application for a licence to serve alcohol there. Considerable discussion followed about unnecessary competition with the hotel, and it seems it was situated nearby on Flamborough Road. There was, after all, an Alexandra Laundry close to the rear of the hotel. Perhaps clever entrepreneurs were simply cashing in on the reputation of this nearby high class hotel, and naming their businesses accordingly?

One thing is certain, however. We cannot assume running a large enterprise like The Alex was ever easy. In September 1868, just two years after it opened, the hotel confidently advertised it could offer "good stabling and coach house, pony carriages, carriage, wagonette, cubs and dog cart all let out for hire." (A cub cart was a handcart pushed by boys to and from the railway station.) Yet only three years later trouble was brewing.

In 1871, the owner-manager, Edwin Taylor, had to sell eleven of his "very superior horses" kept at Beverley Stables, along with his other two hotels (The Crescent Hotel, Filey, and The Great Northern Hotel, Lincoln). In February it was announced that The Bridlington Quay Alexandra Hotel Company was to be liquidated, and creditors were advised to contact the solicitors. Obviously, running a large hotel in the 1870s was as precarious as it was a hundred years later in the 1970s when The Alex finally closed, its owner declaring bankruptcy.

Quite apart from the demands of the enormous building, managing a large staff efficiently would also have its difficulties. For example, in 1889 Mrs Pailthorpe, the manager of the hotel, took one of the cooks to court for stealing eight linen sheets. The cook was Margaret Matters, aged 87! That raises so many questions: she was alive when people like Napoleon Bonaparte and Lord Nelson were making the news. Why was that very elderly lady still working at that great age? Had she stolen before? Did she even know what she was doing? Was stealing by staff rife, and was she being made an example to others? Was she found guilty and fined? Did she continue working there? What happened to her? While we know nothing more about her, we will see later that stealing by members of the staff was not unknown throughout the years.

These names and dates can all be confusing as we read them decades later, but what we see is a group of people in Bridlington, all wealthy, all male (a sign of the times!), all adventurous, all entrepreneurs, and all committing large sums of money to new ventures. These included this grand hotel on the coast, as they foresaw this seaside developing from a harbour through a spa town into a bustling resort which could offer visitors refreshment and renewal, and offer them in return a handsome financial profit. These were men caught up in the excitement of the latter half of the nineteenth century, men with a nose for business, an eye to the future, and a heart open also to public service and generous philanthropy. These are men of whom Bridlington had reason to be proud and to be grateful.

7. WHAT'S IN A NAME?

In creating the Alexandra Hotel, no detail was left to chance. The shareholders realised that if they were to offer hospitality of distinction, then the very name must signify that. So why was the hotel called "The Alexandra"?

All around the coast magnificent hotels were being built. To give them a high profile, presumptuous names were often chosen like "The Grand". But what could be better for attracting attention than to suggest a link with the nobility and, best of all, royalty?

The story begins with the wayward son of Queen Victoria and Prince Albert: Edward, Prince of Wales. Victoria had proved to be a tyrannical parent to her nine children once her beloved Albert died, and each child found their own way of dealing with that. Edward proved to be the strong-willed rebel who reacted violently against his mother's strict code of conduct, and spent his time gambling, partying, enjoying countless affairs and generally embarrassing his mother. We shall return to this later when we see a sordid connection with a famous guest at the hotel.

Victoria was very determined to find Edward, as the future monarch, a suitable bride, and Princess Alexandra of Denmark was eventually chosen, but only after all other possibilities had been exhausted. Born in 1844, she was neither rich nor powerful, and her only childhood claim to fame was that Hans Christian Anderson used to read her bedtime stories. When she was aged only sixteen, she was chosen to be Edward's wife. They were introduced in

September 1861, Edward proposed in September 1862 (but only after his latest affair with Nellie Clifden ended), and they married in March 1863 at Windsor. On her marriage, Alexandra took the title Princess of Wales, and held it for a record number of years until 1901.

Her life was a mixture of joy and sadness. She had six children, Albert Victor being the first, born premature in 1864. In fact, all her later children (George, Louise, Victoria, Maud and John) were born premature. However, there was more than a suspicion that she deliberately told Queen Victoria the wrong expected dates to ensure her domineering mother-in-law was not present at the births – royal births had to be witnessed by several people to testify that the baby really was the royal child. During the birth of Louise, Alexandra developed life-threatening rheumatic fever, which left her with a limp. When her last child, John, died aged just one day old, Edward immediately left for an all-male hunting trip to India!

Despite all this, Alexandra proved to be dignified and charming, affectionate and joyful. She loved dancing, ice-skating, horse-riding, tandem-driving and hunting – all despite the fact that she needed the help of a walking stick. She was a keen photographer and always paid great attention to looking youthful. She quickly became very popular and a fashion icon among both the aristocracy and the general population.

Alexandra was strictly excluded from anything to do with politics and state affairs, and while she was Princess, her husband Edward paid her little attention until he contracted typhoid, at which point he ended his cold estrangement and the two became more reconciled.

Edward, however, never treated her well. He had a constant succession of mistresses, including: actress Sarah Bernhardt, Lady Randolph Churchill, actress Nellie Clifden, aristocratic Patsy Cornwallis-West, Daisy Grenville the Countess of Warwick, society hostess Alice Keppel, philanthropist Agnes Keyser, actress Lillie Langtry, Lady Susan Vane-Tempest, actress La Belle Otero, and soprano Hortense Schneider. Yet Alexandra remained faithful and loyal throughout.

Indeed, history has a peculiar habit of repeating itself in strange ways. Prince Edward, Prince of Wales, was the great-great-grandfather of Prince Charles, a later Prince of Wales. One of Edward's favourite mistresses was Alice Keppel, who was the great-grandmother of Camilla Parker-Bowles, with whom Prince Charles was associated and later married. It was Alice Keppel who was widely acknowledged to be one of the few people who could lift Prince Edward's frequent dark moods, and indeed Princess Alexandra became very fond of her. It seems history repeats itself, but different times and different expectations bring about different public responses to graphic reports of royal behaviour.

In 1901, when her husband became King Edward the Seventh, Alexandra took the title "Queen-Empress Consort", which she held until Edward's death in 1910.

Increasingly deaf, she took on many public and charitable duties, endearing herself to her people. Bazaars, concerts, and hospital visits all filled her days and she never seemed to complain. She had no understanding of financial management and gave huge donations to good causes, much to the fury of her advisers. She would often visit Joseph Merrick (the Elephant Man) in the London Hospital, and she devoted herself to her own children who clearly loved her.

When Edward died in 1910 she moved into Marlborough House, also keeping Sandringham for herself, and became known as the Queen Mother. Alexandra became temporarily blind in 1920, and her memory and speech was impaired in later years. She died in 1925.

So what was the legacy of this tragic, misused woman who was catapulted into the public gaze and yet somehow managed to maintain a dignified and beautiful approach to life?

During the Sudan War (1881-99) she collected funds for a ferry for the wounded, named "The Alexandra", and a hospital ship was named "The Princess of Wales". But it was in the Second Boer War which followed (1899-1902) that perhaps her greatest and most significant lasting contribution came. She established "The Queen Alexandra Imperial Military Nursing Service", which later became "The Queen Alexandra Royal Army Nursing Corps". For over a century now these nurses have worked at the sharp end of military life and still honour her as a key person in their founding. The Alexandra Rose Day became a national day of fundraising to help service personnel with disabilities, and those hospitals devoted to their care and rehabilitation.

Her name is everywhere. Given her interest in medical care, it is not surprising there are many "Princess Alexandra" Hospitals throughout the country. The Queen Alexandra Memorial at Marlborough Gate in London was unveiled in 1932, and no fewer than sixty-seven roads and streets in London alone bear her name.

But what is amazing is that her popularity can be traced right back to her difficult marriage to Edward. In north London, a great park was established which was originally to be called "The People's Park". She had married in March 1863 and when the park opened just four months later in July 1863 it was renamed "Alexandra Park". Set within it, Alexandra Palace was built in 1875, and later became the first home of the BBC.

So loved was she that the fashion of a high collar she always wore to hide a scar on her neck became copied everywhere, and people even imitated her limp, known as the "Alexandra Limp". She was simply a national icon, a role model, and a true celebrity.

In Bridlington, none of this went unnoticed, and the shareholders of the new hotel agreed that the "Alexandra Hotel" was exactly the right title to give to their venture. It encouraged a warm, affectionate, bright, generous and hospitable feeling – just right for a hotel ready to welcome its guests to the town.

8. A HYDRO HOTEL

As human beings we have a special relationship with water at a variety of levels. Biologists tell us we are about sixty per cent composed of water. We are nurtured in water before we are born. When starved of it we dehydrate and die very quickly. Water refreshes, restores, cleanses and calms us. Spiritual literature like the Bible is full of references to the central symbolism of water – Moses passing through the Red Sea, Joshua crossing the River Jordan, John the Baptist baptising Jesus in the same river, and Christian baptism itself. In fact, throughout the world water is a powerful symbol common to all religions, all cultures and all races.

If we feel stressed we can sit by water and it feels as if all our troubles can float away. We look at the reflection of the trees and clouds on still water and realise we see them differently – upside-down. In fact, we go to a place of reflection precisely for that: to reflect on life and see things differently.

Water and the sea became increasingly acknowledged as nature's hospital during the eighteenth century. As the years passed, it became fashionable to come to the coast, the purpose initially being not to swim but to bathe, to have a bath. Simply being clean obviously had a novel and beneficial effect for many! Sea-bathing hospitals began to appear around Europe and in 1844 Bishop's Hot and Cold Baths opened near the harbour in Bridlington, boasting its piped sea water. These were demolished in 1860 to make way for the new sea wall but in 1874 George Travis opened his "New Baths" offering a more modern concept: "commodious room...fitted with every modern appliance...Turkish Bath two shillings and sixpence, Russian Bath two shillings, Warm Sea Bath two shillings, Shower one shilling, Second Class one shilling and sixpence"; and all this only eight years after The Alex was built. This was clearly not just a place for a quick plunge in icy water, but a place to relax, be pampered, and be sociable.

Hydrotherapy was a practice invented by Vincent Priessnitz, an illiterate Austrian, in the 1820s. By the 1840s his health resort was very popular and his theories and methods spread quickly around Europe and America. The wealthy flocked to this new "complementary medicine". Priessnitz claimed to have cured himself (though we are not sure of what) by wrapping himself tightly in towels soaked in cold water, and he invited others to try it at his farm in Grafenberg. He also used cold water internally to cleanse the digestive system – colonic irrigation?

In 1870 John Smedley (1803-74) wrote a book five hundred and twelve pages long, entitled "Practical Hydrotherapy Including Plans Of Baths And Remarks On Diets, Clothing And Habits Of Life." Just four years later the booklet was in its fourteenth edition, such was the explosion of interest.

Hydrotherapy developed into a system of plunging into cold water, combined with lots of exercise and fresh air. In the 1860s and 1870s hydro hotels were operating in Pitlochry, Callandar, Torquay, and Hexham. To the south of Bridlington in Hornsea, The Granville Hotel built in 1912 was originally called The Imperial Hydro Hotel, and boasted Turkish Baths and an indoor swimming pool. To the north in Scarborough, The Grand Hotel even had installed an extra pair of taps on each bath for those guests who chose to bathe in sea water piped directly from the bay.

All of this was naturally and freely available at Bridlington. The North Sea, wide open sands, Sewerby Cliff paths, and fresh winds were all in abundance. Florence Nightingale, Charles Dickens, Charles Darwin and Lord Tennyson all championed sea water as life-giving and health-restoring. In fact, right up to his death, Charles Darwin showered daily in cold water from a hose pipe in his garden.

Hydro hotels usually had doctors on hand and opened for longer seasons. They offered medicinal facilities of different sorts such as seaweed baths, vapour baths, and the Alexandra Hotel could not have called itself "hydro" without offering at least some of these experiences on its premises.

Hydropathical hotels might offer Turkish and galvanic and electro-chemical baths. These typically passed very low electrical currents through water heated to 34 degrees Celsius, and claimed to cure ailments such as arthritis. Even today, hand held galvanic spa apparatus can easily be bought with its claims to heal skin complaints and so on.

Economically, hydro hotels seemed a very good idea as they extended the season throughout the year. Through gritted teeth their adverts would claim "no pain, no gain" as they encouraged a swim in the freezing cold sea in winter, after which guests could return to the warm hotel to recover. Ultimately, however, they failed financially. They were often patronised by those with more money than sense and people who could not distinguish a knowledgeable doctor from a charlatan and quack.

But in this era of new ideas, perhaps it is not surprising that we find in some of the photographs and literature of The Alex the title "The Alexandra Hydro Hotel" between the years 1906 and 1911. The Alexandra Hotel had been formally re-registered as The Alexandra Hydro Hotel Company with new owners and this was no casual change of name. It would have been an obvious way to market the hotel. It is no different to the way that today many hotels will advertise themselves as a "spa hotel" by offering a small pool, a sauna, a Jacuzzi together with various alternative health treatments such as massage, hot pebbles, aromatherapy, reflexology and so on. Set in front of the sea with gardens and promenades all nearby, the hotel could offer a holiday which would also allow a visit to the best doctor available – nature itself. The holiday therefore could be justified as a "curative experience" rather than a purely hedonistic indulgence. Guests came to bathe in, to breathe in, and to drink in nature's heath-giving medicine.

With all this in the background, we find a pre-First World War brochure advertising The Alex as a "Hydro Hotel", boasting a lot of facilities which were presumably a result of the 1907 extension and refurbishment. "New sanitary arrangements, three new lounges near the entrance, a new billiard room, a refurnished dining room, every room renovated and redecorated, each floor with bathrooms and lavatories, a lift and electric light in all rooms, nearby livery stables for horses and carriages and cars." This was an expensive refurbishment.

It offers further details of daily rates: "Rooms from nine shillings according to size, in the summer from ten shillings and sixpence. First floor rooms twelve shillings and sixpence to fifteen shillings and sixpence; second floor rooms eleven shillings and sixpence to fourteen shillings and sixpence; third and fourth floor rooms ten shillings and sixpence to eleven shillings and sixpence. Children charged at two guineas to two pounds fifteen shillings per week. A private sitting room ten shillings and sixpence. A fire in the bedroom, one shilling and sixpence per day and one shilling per evening."

Other details include: "no pets or dogs in public rooms: fed at one shilling per day. A dark room is available for amateur photographers."

What is odd is that for all the amenities listed, no mention is made of any specifically "hydro" facilities. We have to wonder, therefore, if the addition of the word "Hydro" to the name of the hotel was simply an advertising gimmick relying on the close proximity of the beach.

But history is strange. For some reason, boredom perhaps, simply floating in the water came to be regarded as "unnatural" and sometimes dangerous. To avoid drowning, or being pulled out to sea by the tides and currents, swimming strokes were deliberately developed – breaststroke, crawl, backstroke, butterfly. Amateur swimming clubs began to appear and races for fun became a sport in which to participate or watch from the promenade or a boat. Acrobatics, diving and speed were all a new water-based entertainment at the seaside.

Gradually, swimming in the sea became a leisure activity rather than purely a physical discipline for good health. People appreciated specially built sheltered lidos with calm and warmer water. In the British climate, enclosed swimming pools with roofs eventually developed as the norm – places of fun, exercise, competition and good company. Perhaps, during the short time in which The Alex was marketed as a "Hydro Hotel", in its own small way it helped to sow the seeds which eventually led to the magnificent Leisure Centre and Swimming Pool which now stands just a few hundred yards away on North Beach?

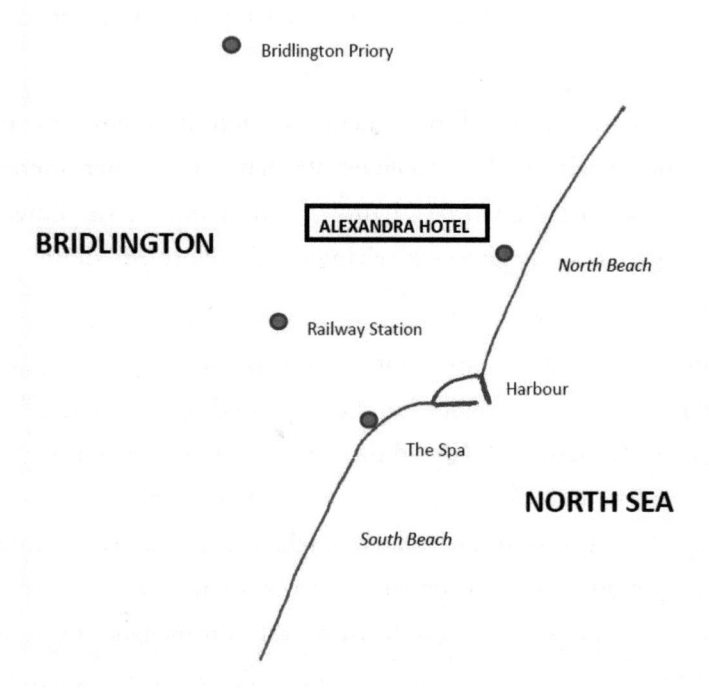

- Bridlington Priory

BRIDLINGTON

ALEXANDRA HOTEL

North Beach

- Railway Station

Harbour

The Spa

NORTH SEA

South Beach

The Alex, set on the edge of both the town and the sea, was ideally placed to market itself as a "Hydro Hotel".

9. APPEARANCES ARE EVERYTHING

Winston Churchill once said, "We shape buildings, and thereafter they shape us," and he was absolutely right. There is no such thing as neutral architecture. The buildings we design all have two purposes. The first is purely functional – maybe a house to accommodate a family, a theatre to accommodate an audience, or a church to accommodate a congregation. The second is more subtle: it is about having a deliberate effect on those who see it, pass by or enter it.

A grand palace with a long drive leading to high steps is deliberately designed to make us feel small – to remind us of our lower place in society. Large doors leading into a large entrance hall have the same effect – they diminish us and keep us humble. A low-roofed bungalow with a single door leading into a cosy hall, on the other hand, makes us feel welcome and significant. Statues of dragons, coats of arms and large iron gates send one deliberately imposing message. Lavender bushes, a pastel coloured door and a welcome mat gently offer a quite different message.

Internally, exactly the same is true. In a person's lounge the arrangement of the chairs, the position of the television and any pictures all make statements about how these people spend their time together and what is important to them. Do they talk a lot or sit passively in front of the screen? What do the pictures of family members or of holidays tell us? Do the ornaments suggest particular hobbies or interests? We deliberately furnish and colour a bedroom, a bathroom and a lounge differently according to what we do in there, so what do the various colours and patterns tell us? Our homes are always a statement about us.

We design our buildings, and then they have an effect on us. They enhance or diminish us, they comfort or disturb us, and they bring us together with people or separate us from each other. In short, the buildings that we shape then shape our emotions, self-esteem, activities and even our sleep patterns. Churchill was absolutely right, and the architect who designed the Alexandra Hotel, W. B. Stewart of Scarborough, clearly knew all this.

The Alex was designed to dominate the North Beach of Bridlington. It could be seen from Flamborough Head in the north to beyond the harbour in the south. It sat solid and square facing the sea stating very clearly: "I am here and here to stay." It was large, imposing and deliberately dominant. No other building along the shore could match it. It was always meant to be the pride of the town, a symbol of aspiration that offered exclusive accommodation. Those visitors who could stay in this prime hotel would be recognised as those with the most money and the most taste. It was all about status. The message was easy to read: here is luxury accommodation in opulent surroundings for those who can afford it.

It was built to command a magnificent panoramic view over the North Sea (the German Ocean as it was then called), offering four acres of pleasure gardens and direct access down private steps to the beach where bathing huts and Corporation beach tents could be hired. Immediately behind the hotel stood a livery stable, initially for horses and carriages and then later for motor cars. Visitors who took boat trips out from the harbour were meant to look back from the ocean and marvel at it as it stood sure and defiant against the elements.

The whole concept came just at the right time. The profession of "architect" was a relatively new one to be publicly recognised, with the establishing of professional bodies coming in 1834, in particular, the Institute of Royal Architects, which in 1837 was renamed The Royal Institute of British Architects.

The newly laid railways made it possible to bring different building materials quickly and cheaply. Slates now often replaced local tiles and new developments such as iron–framed buildings, plate glass, terracotta and polished granite became conveniently available. The Alexandra Hotel was very obviously a child of this railway age.

The first half of the nineteenth century was still dominated by the old classical and formal styles of architecture for public buildings, but became challenged in the middle of the century by the Gothic Revival. This became the chosen favourite for the new Houses of Parliament in 1834, and Gilbert Scott championed this with his many churches (including the restoration of Bridlington Priory in the 1870s), the Albert Memorial and St Pancras Station in London. It allowed architects to collaborate with artists and sculptors to create more ornate features and styles of doorways, windows, towers and turrets. Extravagance, civic pride, solidity and cutting-edge fashion would all have appealed to the shareholders in Bridlington who were demonstrating modern and bold entrepreneurship in their project. They grasped the opportunity with both hands, and took full advantage of this new architectural freedom which somehow seemed to reflect the very freedom of the sea itself.

Fashion, economics, location, climate, and available technology all combined in favour of The Alex. Solidly rectangular, facing east, it had five storeys, and the ground floor windows of the public rooms were all tall with rounded arches. Higher windows became progressively smaller with each storey to give a sense of stability and perspective. When it first appeared, it must have seemed monumental in scale, standing defiant against the winds and the waves of the North Sea.

On each corner was a squat square turret and the roof had an iron palisade all around it. Flagpoles adorned the turrets and the centre of the roof above the main door. The entrance was up a few steps set within an ornate porch supported by carved pillars. High above the central main door near the roof was a carved stone feature showing a monogram with the intertwined letters "AH" for "Alexandra Hotel", set between two winged cherubs. To stay here would be stately and heavenly!

On the ground floor the public areas were very spacious – a large entrance hall to make it clear that visitors were entering somewhere very grand. This entrance lobby was the only public space where any semblance of busyness would be seen: cases carried by porters, keys given, lifts operated, requests made, advice sought, carriages ordered, and bills paid. But even then an air of calm competence would be the order of the day.

Open-plan lounges led off the wide corridors, with seating arranged easily and casually. Parlour palms and oil paintings gave an air of homely comfort, and the carpets and wallpaper were all sumptuous gold and red. Pillars along the corridors gave an atmosphere of aesthetic grandeur and elegance. Fireplaces were everywhere, and outside chimney pots were visible and clustered to show others that there was a hotel which offered cosy and warm hospitality, and every room had its own fireplace. Indeed, in all buildings the number of chimney pots was an indication of the wealth and status of the owner.

The dining room could eventually seat three hundred and fifty and the ballroom could accommodate three hundred dancers. There was a billiard room, drawing rooms, smoking rooms, and in later years even a dark room for amateur photographers.

Staircases were broad and easy, becoming increasingly narrow only as one progressed from floor to floor. All seventy-two bedrooms had a fireplace and a sink, with bathrooms and toilets on each floor. Suites could be reserved for families. Meals could be served in private rooms as desired.

Experienced cooks were hired to provide excellent and varied cuisine, and the kitchens were positioned far away from the public rooms to keep the smell of cooking from the guests. In later years, it became a source of grumbling that the food served was always cold because it took so long to bring it to the dining room!

Refinement, elegance and contemporary comfort were all combined to offer a stay in "another place". This was not to be just any boarding house by the seaside. It was a trip into a fantasy world, just as much as a trip to Disney World is today, or a stay in a multi-star hotel in Dubai. The architecture within and without all proclaimed loud and clear that here you would be transported into another world, so that returning home you feel better in yourself and about yourself. This was hospitality in the truest sense of the word. It was to be a hospital for the body, the mind and the soul.

An early drawing of Trinity Cut and Bridlington from the site not yet occupied by the hotel.

Trinity Cut and the new houses on Sewerby Terrace before the hotel was built.

North Beach Cliffs before the hotel and the seawall were constructed.

North Beach before the sea wall was built. The new hotel can be seen in the background.

The new hotel can just be seen in the distance, towering above the new developments along North Beach.

Work begins on the new sea wall on North Beach.
The hotel can just be seen in the distance.

Nearby Marlborough Terrace (dated 1871) five years after the hotel is completed.

Smart houses were soon developed along North Beach to complement the hotel.

An early drawing of the hotel in the 1890s.

Alexandra Hotel
BRIDLINGTON

A stylised drawing of the hotel from an advertisement.

The hotel in 1895.

The monogram with an interwoven A-H for "Alexandra Hotel" sat in the centre of the roof-line, with cherubs supporting it each side – proclaiming a "heavenly holiday"?

An early advertisement boasting the new and prestigious telephone number – "Bridlington 1" of the recently renamed "Hydro" Hotel.

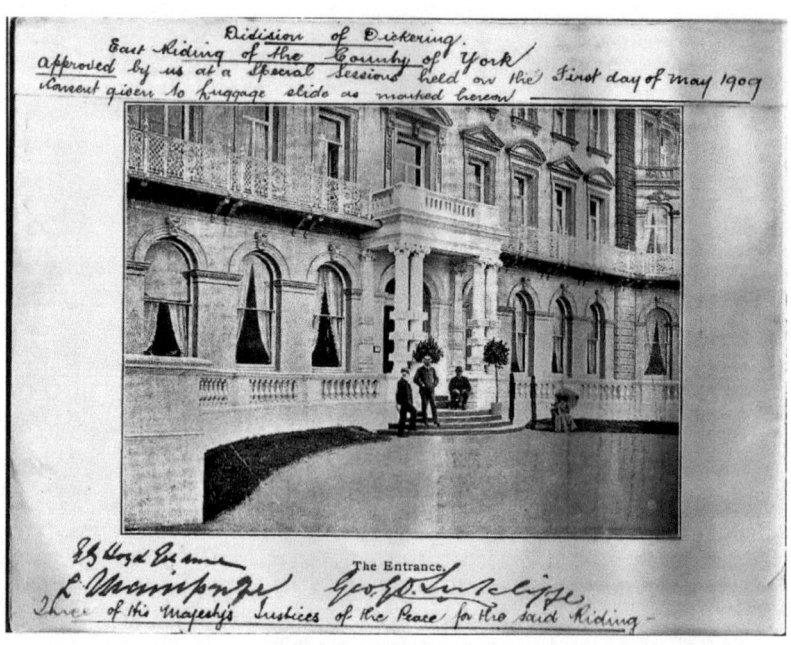

The hotel porch, 1909.

The new hotel stands proud and defiant overlooking the beach.

Bishop's Baths near the harbour helped pioneer bathing for health, and not just pleasure. The hotel is in the right corner peeking over the roofs.

From Trinity Bridge, the new hotel offers a calm oasis.

The hotel's sea-facing patio and mature gardens.

Corridore.

An early photograph of a downstairs corridor, complete with columns, sumptuous carpets and wallpaper.

Another of the Lounges

An early photograph of one of the lounges. Note the parlour palms, a favourite of the time.

An early photograph of the billiard room and smoking room.

An early photograph shows the quiet, relaxed atmosphere in one of the lounges

An early photograph of the original dining room.

An early photograph of one of the bedrooms, complete with potty under the bed! Hardly luxurious by today's standards

Princess Alexandra, after whom the hotel was named.

Alexandra as Queen Consort with Edward VII.

Alexandra Palace in London, named in honour of Princess Alexandra.

The uniform of the Alexandra Nurses.

A picture of the hotel as a "Hydro Hotel", 1907.

The Hydro Hotel in its early days.

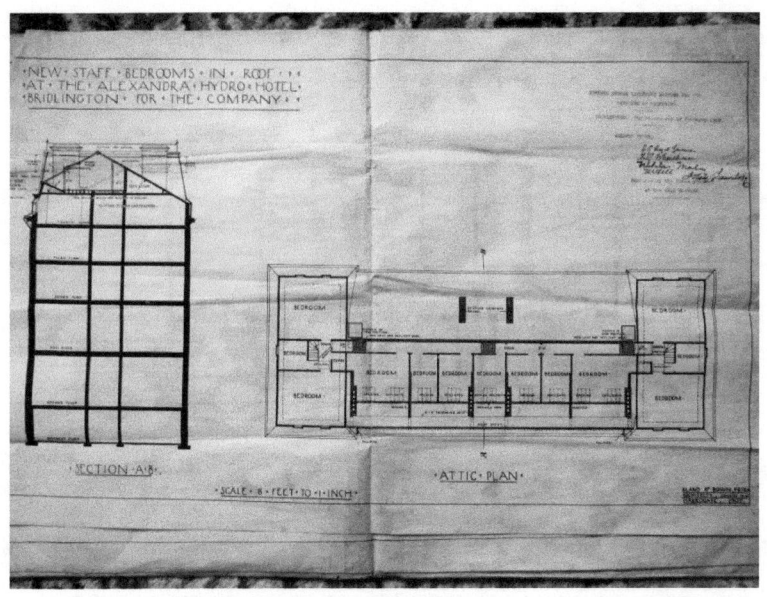

Plan of the 1907 addition of staff bedrooms in the attic.

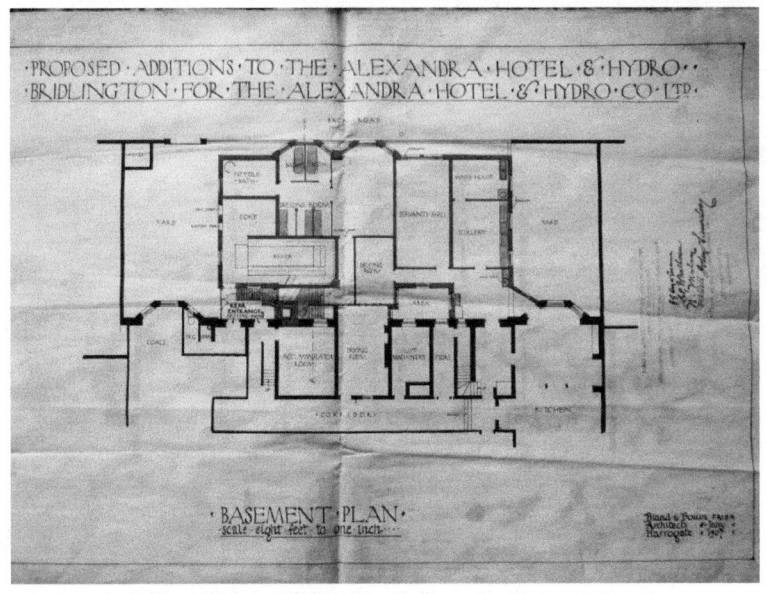

Plan of the 1907 extension to the basement.

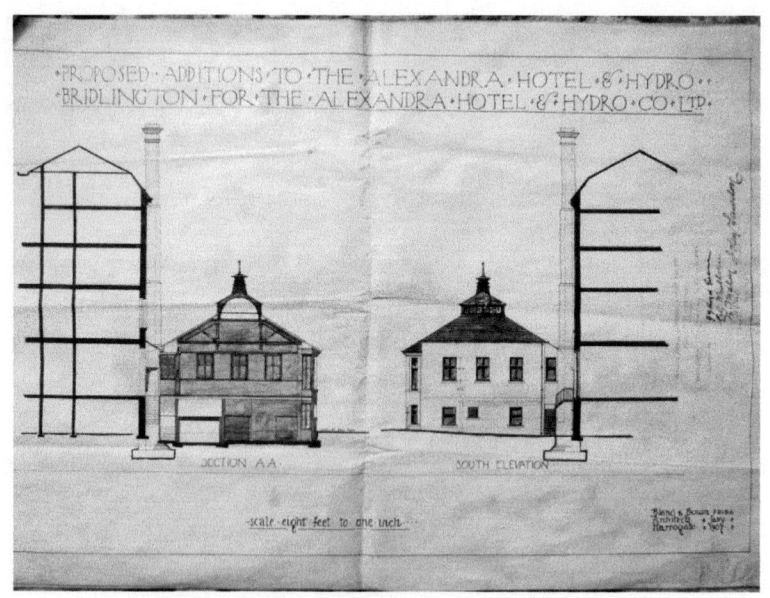

Plan of the 1907 extension from the south side.

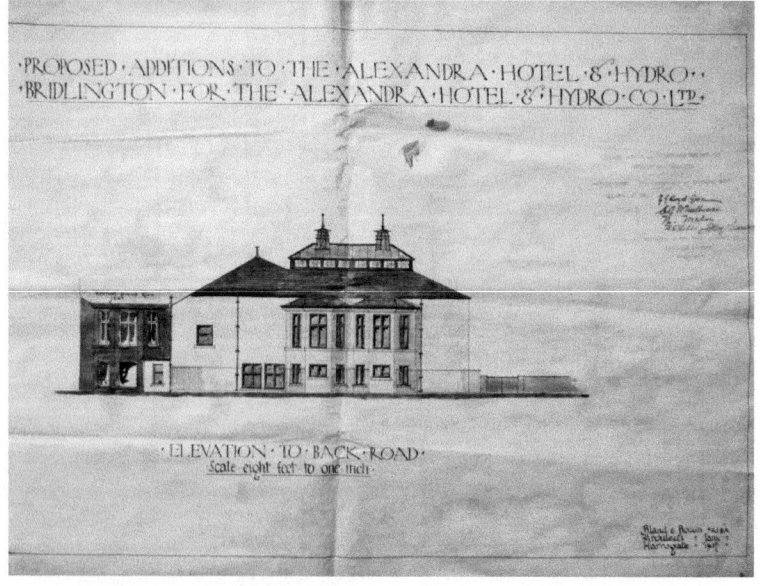

Plan of the 1907 extension to the rear of the hotel.

New and Up-to-Date Electric Lift to all floors just added by Messrs. Waygood & Co., London.

View of the Hydro from the Sea.

In 1909 a new Waygood electric lift was installed, saving guests and staff climbing all those floors.

Scarborough Town Hall, also designed by the hotel's architect, W. B. Stewart.

Westborough Methodist Church, Scarborough, also designed by the hotel's architect W. B. Stewart.

10. ARE THERE ANY DETECTIVES OUT THERE?

Detective stories are always popular whether in books, on stage, on television or in the cinema. Whether it is a Sherlock Holmes story, an Agatha Christie plot or the latest Hollywood spy thriller, we seem to have an insatiable appetite to find out what really happened, who did what and when, and why and how.

But solving real-life historical "whodunnits" can be notoriously difficult as evidence has a habit of disappearing, whether through being deliberately concealed or accidentally destroyed. We can find following the trail of clues both confused and confusing. This is precisely the case with one aspect of the development of The Alex as a building.

Here is the question: when did the two ground floor extensions, one on the north side and one on the south side, appear? In the north extension was the enlarged dining room, and in the south extension were the ballroom and other smaller rooms. It probably helps to follow the confusing and partial trail of clues by looking at the relevant photographs.

The evidence presented to us appears to be:

Pre-1864: In early sketches some large terraced town houses stand at the entrance of Sewerby Terrace, a little distant from the site of the hotel, on the south side.

1864-6: The seventy-bedroomed hotel is built and is shown in various undated sketches and photographs standing alone, some distance apart from the first houses in Sewerby Terrace.

1880-1910: The hotel is advertised in local newspapers in Sheffield, Lincoln and Nottingham boasting a large number of rooms. Curiously, the number advertised varies from seventy, to seventy-two, to over one hundred, to over one hundred and fifty. This could be simply that the management sometimes advertised the number of bedrooms, and sometimes the total number of rooms – bedrooms, public rooms and staff rooms – to emphasise its grandeur. Brochures from the 1960s and 1970s advertise the number of bedrooms as around seventy.

1890: Dated photographs show the hotel now with town houses built terraced onto each side of the hotel, on the south side filling completely the gap between the original houses in Sewerby Terrace and the hotel. These are described as guest houses which could each accommodate twelve to fifteen visitors. Was the land originally owned by the hotel and were the houses themselves originally owned by the hotel, or not?

1907: Plans exist showing proposed enlargements and some internal reordering, but the plans are incomplete and seem to suggest any extensions were to the rear and not the sides.

1909: A dated photograph shows the houses still attached to each side.

1910: A dated photograph again shows the houses still attached to each side.

1911: A detailed street map shows the hotel with four terraced houses attached to each side of the hotel.

1928: Here is the heart of the mystery. From this date onwards photographs now show the hotel with the houses each side demolished, and two ground floor side extensions built. One (frustratingly) undated photograph shows the new wings under construction. So at some point between 1911 and 1928 the two ground floor extensions were built. But when? It is surely unlikely to have been during the years of the 1914-18 war, so was it between 1911 and 1914 or between 1918 and 1928?

1928: One detailed street map shows the hotel with its new ground floor wings, but now with two rather than four houses each side. In other words, two houses each side had been demolished to make way for these extensions. How easily negotiated was this? Again, did these houses originally belong to the hotel, and was this why they were demolished seemingly without too much difficulty? The photograph showing the extensions under construction also shows the marks of the demolished houses (floors and walls) on the next remaining house.

1920: A plan and drawing for a huge proposed extension by Mr Percy Newbound, then the owner (which never happened, as we shall see later), shows a front elevation which would have required further demolition of more houses. Close inspection of the drawing of the elevation suggests that new rooms on the ground floor to each side of the hotel have high arched windows, which look remarkably similar to those which are in the new completed wings.

So: were the two wings built before 1920, and was Percy Newbound's scheme an ambitious expansion of them?

Or, and this seems more likely: were the two wings all that were built from the 1920 proposals? After all, the proposed massive enlargement was always intended to be phased, and the photographs showing the construction of the wings shows girders extending vertically above the roof as though more was intended.

To suggest that the two wings were all that were built of Percy Newbound's grandiose scheme would fit with his constantly over-ambitious plans for life generally (of which, more later). It would also fit with the fact that he had great ideas for the tourist trade of the town, but which evaporated after the calamitous fire of 1923 which destroyed his nearby Floral Hall. It also explains the very large measurements of the ballroom and the dining room in the 1924 auction brochure (of which, again, more later). So, to suggest a date between 1920 and 1928 would seem likely, with perhaps 1920-1923 as the most likely.

However, all this is pure conjecture based on incomplete evidence. If there are any detectives out there who know how to discover more clues to solve this mystery, the case remains open waiting for answers.

11. MORE THAN JUST A GARDEN

The large front lawn covering almost four acres was no accident. At a practical level, of course, it offered a significant distance between the hotel and the ever threatening waves of the North Sea. It set a large, beautiful and well-manicured boundary demonstrating mastery and defiance over the rages of a sometimes angry ocean which could devour land and in which people could be swept out and drowned.

But the extensive gardens at the front of the hotel were so much more than that. From Victorian times to today, many people have aspired to a home which has at least a small back garden for children's games, barbecues, clothes-drying, and growing some flowers, fruit and vegetables. If there is a front garden, so much the better, but its purpose is quite different.

Ancient stone-age cave dwellers did not grow grass at the front entrance to their homes. In medieval times peasants had no spare land to use simply as an ornament, as every square inch was needed for cultivating food or keeping a few animals. It was only after the middle ages that the extremely rich and powerful, the aristocracy who lived in castles and fortified mansions, began to plant lawns at the entrance to their homes. A lawn was a mark of nobility, and the larger the lawn, the more spare wealth you displayed, and the more noble you appeared. The front lawn and any gardens in them were a clear status symbol.

Ornamental front gardens in stately homes, as opposed to purely functional back gardens, could also be settings for important events such as festivals, celebrations and significant declarations, but only at such designated times were people allowed to walk on the grass. Even today, "Keep off the grass" is a sign still used to make it clear who owns this land, and it is not you!

With the industrial revolution, new money made by the moguls of industry allowed the richer middle classes to build homes with not only a functional back garden, but also a significant front garden. The bigger it was and the longer the driveway to the front door, then the more important was the owner. Bankers and lawyers and merchants all aspired to a good front lawn. Even today in any suburban street, the size, condition and floral arrangements in the front garden all say something about the occupants – and today all streets have their pecking order, decked as they are with statues, ponds, lights, paving, and plants and flowers from the local garden centre.

The front lawn at the Alexandra Hotel was no different. The owners bought into this philosophy wholeheartedly and had the front gardens beautifully landscaped. At first, photographs dated between 1890 and 1910 show curved and wavy paths for promenading, winding around mature bushes and carefully tended flower beds. Seats were arranged and cover offered as guests took their tea in the warm sunshine or the invigorating breeze.

Photographs dated 1910 show a statue of Pandora in the grounds. This life-size figure was a representation of a famous legendary Greek woman. Her name means "all gifted", and according to Greek myth she was the first human woman created by the gods, Hephaestus and Athena, on the orders of Zeus. Each god helped to create her by giving different gifts. She was moulded from earth and the gifts given to here were all seductive in different ways. According to the myth, Pandora opened the box she held (sometimes called "Pandora's Box") and released all the evils of humanity, leaving only Hope inside once she had closed it again. As a myth (a story with a truth), it was an attempt to explain how human beings came into being, why there is so much evil in the world, and hope is in such short supply.

It may seem a strange statue to choose to place in front of the hotel, but stranger still is how it came to stand today in the Rose Garden at Sewerby Hall. No one seems quite clear about how or when it was moved, but it does seem very likely that it is the same statue, given the fate of the hotel gardens over later decades. Perhaps Bridlington Town Council acquired the statue when it bought the front gardens in 1963?

It is even more strange that no records exist with either the Town Council or Sewerby Hall about how or when or why the statue of Pandora now stands in the Rose Garden, and there are others who have a different theory. Some think that the hotel's statue was bought and taken to the eighteenth century country house, Haisthorpe Hall. This imposing home stands off the A104, just four miles from Bridlington, near Carnaby. However, here again there is neither any documentary nor photographic evidence available, so the mystery remains just that – a mystery.

Very naturally, those managing The Alex capitalised on these extensive grounds whenever possible. For example, in the summer of 1888 (self-styled) Professor Wilson's Band played on the front gardens on Monday, Wednesday and Friday evenings. Family tickets were available at one guinea for the year, eight shillings and sixpence for a month, and four shillings and sixpence for a week.

Looking at successive but often undated photographs of the gardens, there appears to be a gradual but deliberate scaling back of the ornamentation, presumably reflecting the decreasing amount of money available for non-essentials as the hotel declined.

The earliest photographs show gardens with expansive sweeps and manicured flower beds. As the years go by there seem to be fewer flower beds and these simply have rose bushes, with more plain lawn. The auction documents of 1924 list no fewer than eight tennis courts. At that time there was a national craze for the sport, which was seen as fashionable, healthy and fun. Fred Perry was the household name with his amazing run of tennis championships, and all hotels with large grounds quickly accommodated new courts. This was a sport for both men and women in an age when, after the First World War, women began to enjoy a new freedom and equality with men having proved their worth in the factories, farms and offices. Needless to say, courting on the tennis courts was never far from the minds of the young and energetic!

Then in photographs dated from 1928 onwards, the tennis courts no longer appear in photographs, and it seems there was just pitch and putt alongside a croquet lawn and finally just plain grass. In the 1940s and 1950s donkey rides were offered to children around the perimeter path, and towards the end the gardens had become just open lawn.

The front garden, as always, is not simply just there by accident. It is a very revealing indication of the economic fortunes of the owner, but the appearance of the tennis court and the mini golf course was not all negative. To be able to advertise a hotel with sporting facilities was a clever move in an age when physical activity for its own sake was growing in popularity.

However, these changes did not mean the gardens had lost their purpose. Each year the hotel continued to host a number of functions, including the annual Garden Party held by the Ladies' Lifeboat Association. In 1963, this was opened by no less a celebrity than the pop star Adam Faith who was performing at the Spa at that time. Indeed, it seemed to become a tradition that the star act of the season would open the garden party. Other nationally famous Spa headline acts to open these annual events included top comedian Benny Hill, television presenter Hughie Green, singer Ronnie Hilton, and entertainer Jimmy Clitheroe, "The Clitheroe Kid". We will meet more famous entertainers later, as guests of the Tiffany family who owned the hotel in the mid-1960s.

Behind the scenes, however, everything was not always straightforward. Originally, the hotel owned all the land almost down to the beach. Eventually, on 5th November 1878 Edwin Taylor (the owner of the hotel) together with the Liberator Building Society (which presumably had lent money in a mortgage) agreed with Bridlington Town Council that there was a legal right of way along the foreshore from the harbour to Sewerby. The footpath had been washed away by the sea and the town council wanted to build a new footpath on hotel land. The agreement was that as long as the council protected the hotel with an effective sea defence, then land would be given for a footpath. So land was given for a promenade, with the legal condition that nothing could be built on it higher than the level of the gardens. Nothing was to impede the view of the sea for the guests.

On 29th June 1923, the town council wrote to the Floral Hall demanding that its advertising boards be removed from in front of the gardens, presumably put there because the hotel and the Floral Hall had one and the same owner, Mr Percy Newbound, of whom more later! On 29th June 1927, the hotel proposed some improvements to the seafront and offered twelve hundred and fifty square yards of frontage to widen the footpath, on condition the council improved the bank of soil with bushes and plants.

The following year, 1928, saw an agreement ratifying an annual payment of two shillings and sixpence by the hotel, and adding that wooden railings were to be added at the top of the slope, with no advertisements of any sort ever to be fixed to the fence. However, on 3rd July 1931 the town council wrote to the hotel manager complaining that illegal advertisement boards had appeared and they should be removed forthwith. The advertisements were for the café services offered by the hotel tearoom on the lawn. Front gardens yet again reveal a lot about the state of affairs of the building behind. But the story does not end there.

In December 1963 there was a constant flow of letters between the hotel and the Town Clerk. By this time the hotel was struggling financially, and an offer had been received to buy the café and kiosk on the lawn together with a small strip of land by Trinity Cut. The hotel wondered if the Corporation might be interested in buying about two acres of the land. The Town Clerk replied that the

Corporation was interested, and noted the original Covenant on the land which stipulated (15th January 1866) that the land should: "forever be kept as open space for recreation and amusement, that nothing taller than four feet in height should ever be built or grown on it, that only fences or seats or ornamental plants were allowed, that it was to be kept in good order and securely fenced, and that no cattle should be allowed on it." After a lot of negotiating (including the town council offering £35,000 for all the land including the hotel), the front gardens alone were bought by the town council for £9,000. After the hotel closed in 1976, the gardens were used for a few years by the Alexandra Bowling Club before it moved to its own new site overlooking South Beach.

It is a sad tale reflecting the slow decline of the hotel as it lost the ability to maintain its original grandeur. Gradually as the gardens were simplified to reduce costs, negotiations dragged on about strips of land and fences, and finally the hotel had to sell the gardens to raise some capital in an attempt to carry on.

Today, the steps down to the promenade and beach, and the steps from the site of the tearoom down to Trinity Cut, are the only remaining pieces of hotel construction, but the grassed lawn continues as a welcome open expanse along the foreshore, ensuring no further development will be crammed into the space. Indeed, this green grass is an important feature of the seafront. Green has long been recognised as having great healing power. It is the most restful colour for the human eye, being at the opposite end of the spectrum to red, the most emotionally charged colour. It is not that the colour green gives our eyes a break, but rather that it gently and measurably calms us emotionally.

None of this should surprise us about the emotional as well as the visual importance of the front gardens of The Alex. One of the original shareholders to invest in the building of the hotel was R. N. Beauvais. He was a churchwarden at the Priory Church for twenty-seven years and a very generous benefactor towards its restoration. His Christian faith was obviously important to him, and as a man who was in church every Sunday, the stories of the Bible would have been second nature to him. He must surely have realised that the picture language of gardens is used to describe both the origin and the ideal destination of all human beings. Adam and Eve and the beginnings of the human race are set in a pleasant garden, the Garden of Eden. Then, recapturing that imagery, just before he died Jesus used the Greek word "Paradise" for Heaven, a word meaning literally a landscaped garden. The notion is that a pleasant garden is a good symbol of a place in which we feel at ease and at peace, our beginning and our end. In the nineteenth century it was no accident that the original owners of The Alex devoted so much space to a landscaped therapeutic garden, and today it is still no accident that it remains for the wellbeing of the visitors and residents of Bridlington.

12. THE SEA VERSUS THE LAND

It is a curious thing how soft, malleable water that can trickle through the fingers, is the same water that can beat relentlessly on hard rock and always eventually destroy it. Poets and mystics through the years have employed this as a picture of how gentle love will always ultimately triumph over hard hearts. The battle between soft and hard, gentle and tough seems to be built into the core of our existence.

Every seaside resort constantly tries to manage the battle between the restless sea and the apparently tough immovable land. All around the British coast there is evidence, and constant concern, that the sea always wins. No matter how hard the rock, how high the cliffs, how gentle the weather, the coastline is constantly being eroded, changed and moved. The thousands of fossils to be found just north of Bridlington near Whitby and Port Mulgrave bear witness to this coming and going of the sea. Spurn Point to the south is an ever shifting sandbank, never plotted on two consecutive maps in the same place. Violent storms, tidal surges, and strong undercurrents can scour our beaches revealing artefacts no one knew existed.

One of the golden treasures of the East Yorkshire coast is its wonderful variety of landscape – the long arm of Spurn Point, the flat lands of Hornsea, the towering white cliffs of Bempton, the sweep of Filey Bay out to Filey Brigg, the promontory of Scarborough Castle, the hidden smugglers' caves of Robin Hood's Bay and Staithes, and so the list goes on, endless and fascinating.

Set right at the heart of all this geological variety is Bridlington. It offers to the south of the harbour the vast flat open sands of South Beach, and to the north of the harbour the gradual ascent through Sewerby to the drama of Flamborough Head with its limestone cliffs and hidden bays. Between the harbour and Sewerby, however, are gently rising layers of clay, and these clay risings have always hampered developments and looked unsightly with their constant mud-slides into the sea.

Human beings seem always to have had a need to claim the land as their own, mark it out with fences and walls, and declare their mastery over the soil. At the coast, this mastery has to be demonstrated over the sea as well as over the land. At first, wooden shuttering was driven in place, always only providing temporary respite from the battering waves. At various places, lengths of stone wall were built by private developers, and often people were charged money to walk by these walls protected from the sea. The admission charges had two aims: to recoup some of the costs, and to keep out the penniless riff-raff!

Architects and builders always work to manipulate the environment to the advantage of their clients and the public, and the building of sea walls is a part of that desire to demonstrate a mastery over nature once it has been domesticated and, at the coast, that the sea has also been tamed.

So it was realised from the start that the sloping clay bank in front of the Alexandra Hotel obviously needed attention, or in time the grounds would be eaten away by the tides and currents and the hotel itself endangered.

Consequently, between 1866 and 1869 a length of coast measuring six hundred and ninety feet in front of the hotel was reclaimed and a parade built with flower beds at a cost of two thousand pounds, no small sum of money. Twenty years later in 1886 the sea wall from "Sand's Cut" (now Trinity Cut) extending one thousand feet north was built at the huge cost of six thousand pounds from a plan by Clark and Pickerill (engineers), and in 1887-8 it was extended south from Trinity Cut to Victoria Terrace at a further cost of ten thousand, four hundred pounds. To put these costs in perspective, nearby Holy Trinity Church had been completely built in 1871 for just six thousand, five hundred pounds.

The hotel quite naturally wasted no time making the most of this brand new seaside attraction. On 21st July 1888, an advertisement in The Bridlington Quay Gazette stated: "Tickets may be bought for a grand viewing of the Royal Visit and Opening of the Sea Wall from the grounds of the Alexandra Hotel."

The length in front of the hotel, a private enterprise on private land, was a huge expense for the owners of The Alex, but it did secure the land and offer peace of mind, as well as the opportunity to beautify the gardens, the bank, and the parade with floral gardens and seats. Some of the promenade frontage was developed by Charles Mann with a number of temporary wooden shops and stalls, and was known as "Cheapside", perhaps being the forerunner of those seafront shops which today sell enticingly cheap buckets and spades, snacks and drinks, toys and souvenirs.

Walking along the "Prom" became in itself a relaxing activity for the holidaymaker. An 1882 guidebook describes the promenade along

North Beach which "furnishes a beautiful marine promenade, tastefully enlivened with gay parterres of flowers, ornamental shrubs and everything that can be added to its attractiveness."

The purpose, then as now, was not to rush along to a particular destination, but gently to stroll, take in the salty ozone, enjoy the view, allow the last meal to digest, share some gossip, and parade the latest fashion especially bought for the holiday. Crinoline dresses, ladies' bonnets and gentlemen's frock coats may have given way to blazers and boaters for men and shorter dresses for women, and these in turn may have made way for today's latest trends, but in essence it has remained the same through all the decades. Even today's electric mobile scooters which whizz by are only the latest transformation of the earlier bath chairs so loved by the wives of retired colonels!

With the sea wall safely tried and tested over the years, in order to entice more holidaymakers, the proprietor claimed in 1916 that the hotel was "the finest and the safest hotel on the north east coast." Presumably, this was a deliberate attempt to let people know that although the First World War was raging, Bridlington and its solidly built hotel were safe and open for business.

The widened footpath became known as "Alexandra Promenade" and the gardens just to the south were named "Alexandra Gardens". On this new promenade and in these freshly designed gardens, guests would have paraded themselves in their fashionable clothes made possible by the huge new cotton mills across the Pennines in the ever-expanding industrial cities. Having grown at an enormous speed thanks to new technology, by 1871 Manchester was producing one third of all the cotton goods in the world. Their products were extremely cheap, due in large part to the dreadfully low wages paid to the workers. In that same year of 1871, over two hundred thousand children aged between nine and thirteen were employed in Manchester's mills, none with any of the Health and Safety protection we take for granted today. Their hours were long, discipline was harsh and accidents were frequent. They were the ones paying for the elegance of the parading along the seafront in Bridlington, where young men and women desperately sought new partners, and older couples more calmly sought to impress their friends.

Perhaps creating a memorable impression is what sea walls and seafront promenades are all about. To this day, the unnaturally straight line of the sea wall states quite clearly that human beings have "civilised" the uneven coast of falling rock and mud. But it is an uneasy truce between land and sea. For the time being, the promenade and the gardens are safe, but ultimately the soft malleable water will have its way even with the hardest stone wall, just as surely as the spiritual teacher will keep insisting that gentle but determined love will always eventually conquer a hardened heart.

(iii) HIGH DRAMA

13. LIFEBOATS AND BATHING HUTS

The southern edge of the land owned by the hotel was bordered by Trinity Cut, originally known as Sand's Cut, and now affectionately called the "Donkey Bridge", because the donkeys giving rides on the beach are led down that slipway under the bridge.

The Cut itself appears to have been a natural break in the low cliffs, and early pictures show it as a rough depression overgrown with foliage with a small wooden bridge across it. The present iron bridge was constructed in 1888 after a long and difficult negotiation between Bridlington and Sewerby Councils. The Cut marked the boundary between the two authorities and each claimed the other should carry the whole cost of the bridge. In the end, it was shared equally. The Cut, however, proved invaluable for the hotel, both as the launch site for lifeboats and then as the safe place to store bathing machines.

It is difficult to overestimate the importance of the lifeboats in the history of Bridlington. Between 1770 and 1805 one hundred and seventy-four ships were damaged or completely wrecked by storms. Records show that in 1844 a total of no fewer than seven hundred and sixty-one ships moored for safety in Bridlington Bay, the Bay of Refuge, in addition to all the fishing vessels.

As early as 1805 the first lifeboat house was built on the corner of North Back Street (today called Chapel Street) and Moor Lane. Later, in 1865 (just a year before The Alex opened for business) a new lifeboat house was built at a cost of one hundred and ninety-two pounds on the corner of Railway Crescent (now Windsor Crescent) and Old Hilderthorpe Road, to accommodate the newly arrived lifeboat "Robert Whitworth". The boat with its carriage cost three hundred and ninety pounds, then as now, with huge local financial support. Because the harbour is tidal, the boat had to be taken through town either to North or to South Beach to be launched. If it was to be launched from the North Beach, then it was towed by hired horses to Trinity Cut next to the hotel, or to Sands Lane Slipway, and this all took huge energy and precious time.

Both men and horses were needed for each launch and, for obvious reasons, always in the roughest of weathers. It was and is extremely dangerous work. In 1871, the year of "The Great Gale", the lifeboat "Harbinger" was carried on the shoulders of volunteer men from the boathouse to Trinity Cut for a launch to save lives. Twenty-three ships were driven ashore and nineteen seamen were buried in a part of the Priory churchyard paid for by Captain R. N. Beauvais, one of the founders and original shareholders of The Alex. This tragedy is commemorated annually to this day.

Further launches from Trinity Cut are recorded over the next twenty years, using a succession of lifeboats: "The Seagull", "John Abbott", "William John and Frances", the two "George and Jane Walkers", "Stanhope Smart", "The Tillie Morrison Sheffield" and "The Tillie Morrison Sheffield II".

In 1897 two hundred pounds was contributed by the Lifeboat Institute towards the cost of widening the Cut and laying a stone floor to the slipway. But all did not go smoothly. That same year during a violent gale the wheels of the lifeboat carriage became stuck in the sand and a local journalist, Mr Rogers, was knocked down and killed. The following year, in March 1898 both lifeboats, "Seagull" and "William John and Frances" were wrecked and washed up at Trinity Cut. One of the crew, Christopher Brown, was among those onshore trying to rescue "Seagull" when the boat was smashed against the sea wall and he lost his life. It was obvious this could not continue.

Eventually in 1903 a new lifeboat house was built on South Marine Drive near the Spa Theatre, and Trinity Cut was used less regularly to launch the lifeboat. A photograph dated between 1905 and 1910 has survived showing the "George and Jane Walker" lifeboat being drawn for a launch from Trinity Cut, but judging by the number of very well dressed people and the obvious calm weather, this must have been for ceremony rather than a "call-out". It is probably after one of the large Lifeboat Guild's garden parties on the lawns of The Alex, an annual event which raised thousands of pounds over the years.

Trinity Cut was, however, still sometimes used. There is a record of no fewer than one hundred and fifty men volunteering at nine o'clock in the morning on 22nd December 1909 to pull the lifeboat through town because there was no time to arrange for horses to be hired and draw the carriage to North Beach. That single record is an indication of the importance given to the lifeboat service in the town, and the shared understanding of the vital need for speed and community action. It is not surprising that at the top of people's minds was the question: how can this vital work become more efficient?

Solutions often come from surprising directions. Tractors had proved themselves both on the European battlefields of the First World War and on the farms at home. Consequently, in 1921 there was a trial to pull a lifeboat through town to Trinity Cut by tractor. It took only ten minutes, less than half the time taken by horses and men.

On 5th August 1931, the new lifeboat "Stanhope Smart" was named by Her Royal Highness Princess Mary, Countess of Harewood, and pulled by tractor for a ceremonial launch at Trinity Cut. Its first service launch was on 3rd November that year, again from Trinity Cut.

To this day, the launching of a lifeboat is guaranteed to gather the crowds and be the subject of discussion, concern and press reports. Guests at the hotel would all have had grandstand views from their bedroom windows of every launching of a lifeboat from the Cut, whether it was a launch in desperate weather to save lives, or a ceremonial launch. Both would have drawn huge crowds to watch and pray for safety and success, and each one would have been the main content of animated conversations at the dinner table.

But Trinity Cut was not only the slipway for the early lifeboats. With its cobbled floor what it also did for the Alexandra Hotel was (literally!) to pave the way for the availability of bathing machines for its guests.

As far back as 1715 John Floyer wrote an essay on the benefits of bathing in cold sea water, making a host of bizarre claims about the conditions it could help. But the sea had to be entered, and the question was: how? The answer was the creation of the bathing machine, invented by Benjamin Beale in Margate in the 1730s, with claims that it soon also appeared along the Yorkshire coast around 1735 at Scarborough.

These were usually wooden sheds, about seven feet by five feet, set on wheels, and pulled by a horse into the water. The bather could walk up the steps into the hut on the land side while on the beach, and change into bathing attire while it was moving. Then once in the sea, she could walk down the steps on the seaward side into the ocean. Most had high windows for modesty's sake and some had a canvas tunnel ("a modesty hood") through which to enter the sea so that no bare flesh or bodily shape could be seen. The hood was also invented by Mr Beale, a Quaker, very keen on personal decorum. Sometimes an assistant was on hand to help negotiate the steps.

These machines, although for the rich, were hardly luxurious. Inevitably, they were dark and damp, ill-ventilated and full of sticky salt and sand. Sea water would seep in through the floorboards. Once they were set in motion the occupant was jolted about constantly while trying to get changed.

The maintenance of public morality was seen as very important for the reputation of a town seeking to attract wealthy paying guests. In the early days of the seaside, ladies usually wore loose gowns over large bloomers (invented by the American Women's Rights campaigner, Mrs Bloomer in the 1850s), gathered at the ankle. A cap made from oiled skin might be worn on the head. The men wore bathing suits or bathed naked. By the 1840s the town council had to enforce regulations to prevent "indecencies", and in 1861 a law was passed making nude bathing illegal. Often a rope supported by poles was set in the water to separate areas designated for men and women in order to prevent mixed bathing and "impropriety". Part of the problem was that poorer people had to hire their bathing costumes from the owners of the bathing machines, and these were usually made from cheap serge which sagged and dragged when waterlogged. What the Alexandra Hotel certainly did not want was the poorer classes mixing with their more refined guests on this section of North Beach.

Despite all this, cartoons of the time show men with telescopes watching the women bathe, and the women dressing in such a way to catch their attention. Their costumes began to include corsets to uplift the bust and throw out the bottom in a provocative curve. It is hard to escape the fact that the hotel gardens would have given a grandstand view!

As time went by, however, the fashion in bathing costumes evolved. By 1910 it seems both men and women were generally wearing the same style of one-piece costume which covered them from neck to knee and on the arms down to the elbow. It was only after the First World War, and women taking more control of their lives, that their costumes became closer fitting, with shoulder straps and showing a little cleavage. A short modesty skirt covered their drawers, while men began wearing bathing trunks. Rubber bathing caps became the norm for both men and women. As time went by, and rationing was eased after the Second World War, so silk, rayon and cotton all replaced the old heavy waterlogged woollen costumes of the past. Designs were made to flatter the figure and expose more flesh, encouraged by both Hollywood films and the sunshine of Mediterranean holidays. Today's beachwear is a long way from what those early guests at the Alexandra Hotel would have dared try on as they stepped from their bathing machines into the sea.

These bathing machines could not be afforded by the working classes, and on North Beach they were conveniently stored when not in use in Trinity Cut beside this expensive hotel, The Alex. Brought out each day onto the flat sands in front of the hotel they were an ideal attraction and amenity to be advertised in the hotel's publicity. At first, however, these huts were a source of annoyance as they were not very well organised. Sometimes there were clashes as queues formed while people waited for the last person to finish their swim, get changed, and emerge from their hut. Complaints were frequent about having to wait for most of the morning while affluent and idle women dawdled getting dressed and putting on make-up. Various attempts were made to solve the problem and suggestions included that, instead of paying sixpence per bathe, the cost ought to be per hour and booked in advance, with bookings written in chalk on the side of the hut.

Not only could the working classes not afford these bathing machines, but most of them were only at the seaside for a short time, many for less than a day. They could not waste precious hours queuing and arguing, and most just waded straight into the water. Others preferred to stay on the beach listening to the musicians, watching the Pierrot groups entertain, and patronizing the beach photographers. Fortune tellers, donkey rides and those selling cheap food and drink were usually some distance away from the Alexandra Hotel with its more genteel clientele. The two came together sometimes, however, when those who could not afford to sleep in a boarding house, or were too drunk to find their way home, tried to sleep in one of the bathing huts much to the annoyance of their owners.

By the 1890s canvas bathing tents were appearing on the beach. In these, people could change and simply walk down the beach and into the sea. The bathing machines on wheels gradually became redundant, and often the wheels were removed and the huts placed in a row at the back of the beach, eventually being better decorated and set in rows as beach chalets.

Today, these chalets on both North and South Beach, which are infinitely better built, might have electricity, a water supply, curtains, and quaint decorations offering "home from home" by the sea. But one of their origins was the row of bathing machines used during the day on the beach in front of the hotel, and at night stored in Trinity Cut, which all could be booked by the staff for their guests.

When we recall the uses of Trinity Cut in this way, we see it being used both by the bathing machines to encourage people into the water when calm, and by the lifeboat crews to help people out of the sea when stormy and violent. Those guests staying in the hotel all those years ago will have witnessed both. Perhaps in an unspoken but parallel way, the Alexandra Hotel helped to pull people out of some of the stormy difficulties in their lives at home, and then help them back into calmer waters with a restored and more focused frame of mind. It would be good to think so, for that is the mark of the real hospitality of a true hotel.

14. PLANS FOR EXPANSION – AND A MANICURE!

In its early years, The Alex was often filled to capacity as the town grew in popularity. The vision and enthusiasm of the original developers lived on in those who followed and in 1920 the proprietor, Mr Percy Selwyn Newbound, submitted plans drawn up by the local architect, Mr Percy Bown, F.R.I.B.A. The plans were extremely ambitious.

The frontage was to treble in length to three hundred and sixty-two feet, and the numbers of bedrooms increase to two hundred and twenty. The multi-storey extension of wings to each side of the hotel would have a large ballroom/lounge with dividing screens to allow for different uses. Central heating was to be introduced throughout and the old fireplaces removed. Each bedroom would have a lavatory and a washbasin with hot and cold running water.

The extensions had been designed to allow them to be built in phases using steel frames, concrete slabs and brickwork, and demolishing the current buildings each side as work progressed. Even roof gardens were envisaged in the spaces between the projecting wings on the upper floors.

It was an amazing and brave design, but one which never fully came to fruition. We cannot be totally sure of the reason, but disaster struck. Percy Newbound also owned the Floral Hall on the adjacent Beaconsfield site (where the Premier Inn now stands). It had opened in May 1921 and was a building composed of wood, several old aerodrome hangars having been used in its construction. The theatre could seat over twelve hundred and fifty people with tip-up chairs and there was a picturesque Moorish-style café, served by waitresses in Arabian costume. The architect was Mr Percy Bown, the same architect employed for the proposed extension of the hotel. Tragedy, however, struck on the 25th August 1923 when the Floral Hall caught fire and was burnt to the ground. The performers, auditioning before some London agents, lost most of their belongings and instruments, but mercifully nobody died.

The famous act booked for the following night had to be cancelled: no lesser performer than the star of his day, George Robey. He was simply the greatest music hall performer of his era. Born in 1869, he was a highly talented comedian, singer and actor known as "The Prime Minister of Mirth". In 1916 he popularised the song "If you were the only girl in the world", which became an international success. He moved easily between Shakespearean plays, radio, and later television, and by the time of his death he had raised two million pounds for charity. He was knighted in 1954, the year he died. The sheer fact that he had been booked to play at the Floral Hall indicates the ambition of Percy Newbound and the popularity of the theatre.

When Percy Newbound's dreams for both the hotel expansion and for the development of his entertainment business were dashed, his commitment to the town unsurprisingly evaporated. As we saw earlier, the only part of his plan for hotel expansion to see the light of day was the ground floor extensions between 1920 and 1923. He sold the hotel in 1924 and vowed never to return to Bridlington.

Indeed, looking at his life as a whole, it would seem that for this socially aspiring man, his plan for the Floral Hall, together with a huge hotel offering overnight accommodation for the audience in the next street, may have been just one more over-ambitious enterprise in a whole string of them.

Percy Selwyn Newbound himself was an extremely colourful character. He was born in Hull on 3rd December 1875, the son of Charles Newbound, a bank cashier. He lived with his parents at 14 Arlington Street, Hull, and worked as a solicitor's clerk, his father by then being a cabinet maker. By 1907 he had moved to North Ferriby and that year married Mary Mellers, the daughter of a successful lace manufacturer in Nottingham. They lived in a very fashionable development, The Park, below Nottingham Castle, where stunning homes were built in what was once the castle's deer park. They remain a very desirable address to this day.

This marriage probably provided Percy Newbound with the capital needed for his various ventures – Parkfield (a smart housing estate at North Ferriby), and an involvement with three cinemas in Hull by 1917: The Lyric, The Central, and The Circus. These were not without their complications. In 1916 the Musical Director of the Circus Picture House, Angus Bateman, sued Percy Newbound (the lessee of the cinema) for non-payment of two weeks' wages (£6), after a dispute over who had actually played the music.

He had high political ambitions and stood as a "Non Party, Business and Coalition" candidate in the General Election of December 1918, but he came bottom of the poll with only six hundred and fifty votes.

After the disaster of the Floral Hall fire and the failure fully to extend The Alexandra Hotel, he had moved to London by 1926, and soon afterwards, being an enterprising man reluctant to stand still in life, he took out a patent for a "manicuring appliance". On 28th August 1928 he registered his application for a "Motor Driven Polishing Device For Nails". He described the machine in great detail, offered careful drawings, and included the words: "For polishing the nails by friction – a rotary buffing member of circular form lined with an elastic pad faced with suitable polishing fabric or material (for example, chamois leather) provided with an electric motor. Can be clamped to a table if required." The patent was granted on 16th April 1929, but it is difficult to know if it ever sold or even reached the production stage.

By 1939 he and his wife were living apart: Percy lived at 89 Oxford Gardens, Kensington while his wife Mary lived alone at 22 Queensway, Paddington.

Whatever the high hopes of Percy Newbound were about, perhaps, in the light of the subsequent ebbing tide of tourists, it was just as well the massive hotel extension was never fully built. It is doubtful if it could ever have succeeded financially, but it was a brave try. He was clearly an ambitious, confident, socially aspiring man who seems to have enjoyed big projects which aimed at fame and fortune. Among all the characters of Bridlington he really does stand out as a "one-off".

15. THE 1924 SALE

Throughout the decades the Alexandra Hotel passed through many hands. Owners came and went. Managers came and went. Staff came and went. Perhaps this is an indication that running a hotel of this magnitude is no easy task, and demands more than just initial enthusiasm.

The papers giving details of the sale of the hotel on the 8th July 1924 by Mr Newbound give a fascinating insight into the details of the building. It is described as occupying "an unrivalled position overlooking its own delightful grounds, and commands a splendid view of the North Sea from Flamborough Head to Spurn Point." It "is fully licensed, very comfortable and up to date and in capital decorative order."

On the ground floor is an "attractive entrance and lounge in two bays; Reception and Manager's Offices; Private Offices; Sitting Room; American Bar with separate entrance; small dining room with serving pantry; extensive dining room 86'6" x 42'6" with composition floor and dispensing bar; noble Dancing and Recreation Hall 87' x 42'6" with well-sprung maple floor and a Reception Room adjoining; Still Room and Service Room and Ladies' and Gentlemen's Lavatories.

"On the first floor – eleven bedrooms; Writing Room 43'9" x 24' plus bay; Bathroom; Porter's Bedroom; Ladies' and Gentlemen's Lavatories and Housemaids' Pantries. On the second floor – thirteen bedrooms, Bathroom, Lavatories and Housemaids' Pantries. On the third floor – nineteen bedrooms, Bathroom, Staff Bedroom, Lavatories and Housemaids' Pantries. On the fourth floor – twenty bedrooms, Bathroom, thirteen staff bedrooms. In the basement – extensive Kitchen; scullery; two service lifts; lavatory; Butler's Pantry; numerous Store Rooms; Canteen; Bake-house; Wine, Beer and Mineral Cellars; Men's Quarters; a heated Linen Room; a large Glass and China store; also a Cold Storage with Refrigerator by Kirkcaldy, and a 3hp motor.

"The hotel is heated throughout on the central principle from two 'Ideal' boilers in the basement. Electric light is installed. A quick 'Waygood' passenger lift serves from the ground to the fifth floor. The fourth and intermediate floors are reached by an easy main staircase, and there is also a subsidiary staircase from the basement to the fourth floor. The whole of the furniture, fixtures and fittings will be sold with the property.

"The large open space in front of the Hotel lends itself to the parking of visitors' motors. The delightful Pleasure Grounds are an exceedingly attractive feature and are tastefully laid out and have eight Tennis Courts and broad steps leading to the Marine Drive and restrained on two sides by substantial brick walls, and embankment to the seafront with iron and wood railings.

"The Tea Pavilion in the Lawn is reserved from the sale. The Plot of Land to the rear of the Hotel will be sold with the Property. The stock of all alcoholic liquors, minerals and consumable stores…must be taken by the purchasers at a valuation to be made in the usual way.

"The Estate occupies an unrivalled position being close to the Parade, the Harbour, Pier and principle places of attraction and is within easy reach of the Station and the Spa on the South Bay. Bridlington has attained great popularity as a seaside resort and is governed by an enterprising Council and now has a large residential population; therefore this sale affords a unique opportunity for investors in Hotel property."

(Of all the rooms listed, there is one on the ground floor which has almost disappeared from our sight today – the "Still Room". In medieval times great houses and castles would have a distillery where beer and wine, herbs and medicines could all be stored and used. It was part-pharmacy and part-kitchen, and a vital room for the residents as it held the key to their health and wellbeing. Over time, the "Still Room" developed into the room used by the cook and the housekeeper for storing preserves, liquors, cakes and tea and coffee. It often had in it a gas or electric water boiler and sinks, and might be where cooking pots were kept. A large walk-in pantry, in a hotel like The Alex would have been an important room, and the Still Room Maid would have reported directly to the housekeeper.)

The sale was offered by the owner Mr Percy Newbound whose own great plans for extending the hotel were never fully realised, but the hotel was bought by Mr J. G. Tooth and Mr G. Baxter who had their own plans for upgrading the heating and improving the sports facilities in the gardens.

Other earlier names variously mentioned in connection with the ownership are:

1857	Sale of the land known as 7 Sewerby Terrace to Mr Mark Barr the builder by Mr Robert Walker (presumably as the idea of building a hotel began to be discussed).
1866	Deeds for the Bridlington Quay Alexandra Hotel held in the name of William Duesbury, Thornton Duesbury, Appleby Featon, William Metcalfe, Henry Bainton, and Mark Barr.
1896	Yarborough Harland, Francis Creaser, Sarah Walmsley, Kate Walmsley, Florence Walmsley, Eleanor Walmsley, Gertrude Walmsley.
1906	Arthur Brayshaw and The Alexandra Hotel and Hydro Company (Bridlington) Ltd.
1907	Sarah Johnson, John Graves, Effie Graves, Blanche Johnson, Arthur Stamford, John Wilson.

William Hatje and Isabella bought the hotel in the 1930s, and their fascinating story we will see later.

Stanley Tiffany and his family bought the hotel in 1965 from the Hatje family and, again, we will also see more of their fascinating story later.

Noel and Margaret Crocker bought the hotel in 1967, having previously owned The Castle Hotel in Scarborough.

The last owner was Mrs Margaret Willhelmena (Billy) Compton who had previously run the nearby St Kitt's Hotel, of whom more later.

The details of the physical structure of the hotel suggest three things in particular. First, that there are a large number of rooms devoted to the provision of an exceptionally high standard of service to the guests. Second, that, as pictures of the windows suggest, the largest bedrooms (and therefore the most expensive) are on the lower floors, with bedrooms becoming smaller and with more rooms to a floor the higher one ascended. Third, that a confusing number of names are mentioned in the earlier Deeds of Conveyance. We can only imagine the vast number of meetings, range of emotions, levels of relationships and significance of decisions that were made by those very real people, who were all so much more than just names on historic legal documents.

The lists of names do, however, suggest that a considerable sum of money was required to own and manage the hotel, and that it was often a number of people together who were needed to invest the sum required. On the list of 1896, for example, it appears that four women of the same family were all involved – sisters, mother and daughters, cousins perhaps. That in itself suggests The Alex might have been thinking ahead of its time in already challenging circumstances.

16. TOO WELL CONNECTED?

Among the earliest guests to stay in the Alexandra Hotel were Thomas Wilson and his very large family, in 1868. Wilson was an immensely wealthy, powerful and successful businessman who resided in Park House, Cottingham and lived from 1792 to 1869.

Back in 1822 he and a partner founded the "Beckingham Wilson & Co" shipping line to import iron ore from Sweden for the Sheffield mills. From 1835 passenger ships were added, crossing the North Sea to Hamburg, Rotterdam and Dunkirk. When Beckingham died the company became the "Wilson, Hudson & Co" shipping line. By 1841 it was simply "Thomas Wilson & Sons & Co".

The ships' livery was a trademark red funnel and by 1910 he had over one hundred vessels sailing all over the world with such names as Tasso, Hero, Rolo, Orlando, Eldorado, Romeo, Juno, Aristo, Martebello, Spero, Zero, Salmo, Uno, Calypso, Oslo, Aaro, Eskimo and Bayardo – the names ending in "o" all helping to identify and advertise the company.

Based in Hull, he was a devout church goer and a great philanthropist. He married Susannah West in 1814 and they had fifteen children: David (later a partner in the company), John (the company representative in Sweden), Edward (an engineer), Thomas (a surgeon), Susannah (who married a ship's captain), Elizabeth (who married a shipping agent), Harriet (who married a shipping owner), William, Rachel (who married a corn merchant), Charles (a company partner), Arthur (later a partner), and Emily (who married a corn merchant).

Among these children, Charles was extremely successful in running the company. He was Sheriff of Kingston upon Hull in 1870, the Liberal MP for Hull from 1874 to 1885, and was High Sherriff of Yorkshire in 1891. He became the first Baron Nunburnholme and married the great-niece of the Duke of Wellington. He died in 1901.

Another son, Arthur, was also very successful at running the company after his brother died. He bought three thousand acres of land in the East Riding and was Master of the Holderness Hunt. He was a great philanthropist and was Chairman of the Victoria Children's Hospital in Hull. He died in 1907.

Reading all this, it would seem that, even as early as the 1860s, Thomas Wilson was far too grand to be staying at the Alexandra Hotel. His son Arthur was even able to host Prince Edward, the Prince of Wales, husband of Princess Alexandra, during Doncaster Race Week in his home at Tranby Croft, Anlaby in 1890. It was on this occasion that a terrible scandal broke bringing huge embarrassment to the royal family – of which more later.

Grand hotels were built to appeal to the more snobbish elements of society. While the working classes with their noisy children were seeking rooms in boarding houses in towns, wealthy industrialists were searching for hotels slightly apart from all this. They wanted hotels where children were seen and not heard, and given meals separately by the nannies of the hotel. The standards of the hotel would be expected to match or even surpass those at home, but all this had to become known through both advertising and word of mouth.

The reputation and economic survival of any hotel obviously depends on its ability to attract paying guests. Could it be possible that Thomas Wilson was invited to stay at the Alexandra Hotel for free, as a friend of the shareholders, in order to advertise the prestige of the place? After all, a small town like Bridlington set on the remote east coast of Yorkshire has always worked through connections, both within and beyond itself, that might often be hidden from view. For example, Mr Beauvais and Mr Prickett (original investors and directors of The Alex) were both leading Freemasons in the town, and named Freemasons keep appearing throughout the entire history of the hotel.

For example, amongst others, the architect, W. B. Stewart, was a member of the St John Costorphine Masonic Lodge in Scarborough. Thomas Wilson's son, Charles, later lived at Warter and became first Baron Nunburnholme (very near Londesborough). The locally named Londesborough Lodge of Freemasons was founded in 1858, with its first Worshipful Master being Lord Londesborough. In 1860, his son was elected as the second Worshipful Master, and meetings were held in the Victoria Rooms, Garrison Street, until 1875 when the Londesborough Lodge premises were completed. The Lodge held its centenary meeting in the Alexandra Hotel on 6th June 1958, and to date has admitted over six hundred members.

If there was a masonic link between shareholders, architect, and Wilson and his family, which is purely conjecture but very natural, could this be the link and explain why such a hugely powerful and rich man should grace the hotel with his presence? We may never know, but conspiracy theories are always fun!

17. A ROYAL SCANDAL

Thomas Wilson's association with the Alexandra Hotel, however, was not without its risks. His very successful son, Arthur, lived at Tranby Croft, Anlaby (later a school) near Hull. On 9th September 1890 the Wilson family played host in their luxurious mansion to no less a celebrity than the Prince of Wales, the future King Edward VII. The grand house was their base during Doncaster Race Week. By this time Edward was forty-nine years old and a father of five, but he loved gambling on anything from cards to horses.

That evening in 1890, at what was then an illegal game of baccarat, one of the players, Sir William Gordon-Cumming, was accused of cheating, and accused again the following evening. When confronted, he agreed never to play cards again in return for the promise not to make the matter public. Had it become publicly known, the Prince of Wales would have been severely compromised for breaking the law in participating in the game. The game of baccarat was declared illegal because Parliament decreed it was a game of pure chance and a thousand pounds could be lost easily in just twenty minutes.

But the secrecy did not hold, and Sir William brought a libel action against the Wilson family. The Prince of Wales was forced to give evidence in court – the first time an heir to the throne had been forced to do this since 1411. It became a national scandal.

Sir William himself was a decorated lieutenant. He was a colonel in the Scots Guards and had served in South Africa, Egypt and Sudan.

He often made his house in Belgravia available to the Prince of Wales for his assignations with his many mistresses. He was, himself, a habitual womaniser and shared several of the Prince's mistresses at various times including Lillie Langtry, Sarah Bernhardt and Lady Randolph Churchill.

Surrounding the prince was a fashionable clique known as "The Marlborough House Set", named after his house overlooking The Mall, and comprising members of the old aristocracy together with the new wealthy industrialists such as Arthur Wilson.

The great fear around the case was that by this time Prince Edward had kept over fifty mistresses, and evidence about both his gambling and his adulteries would be reported in the press all over the world. The Prince's reputation was at its lowest point ever.

After the court case, Sir William was forced to resign from the Guards, and the Wilsons held no more glittering functions at their home. Their family fortune declined and Tranby Croft was sold in the 1950s to become a school. The wood-panelled room where the game of baccarat was played remains intact!

What is ironic is that Prince Edward was married to Princess Alexandra, after whom the Bridlington hotel was named. This was the elegant and beautiful princess who tolerated her husband's behaviour, displayed complete discretion, and yet the Wilson family, brought in to give the hotel a reputation for respectability, showed itself to be a very risky association indeed.

18. A LESS RISKY GUEST

Another very early guest, in 1868, was Edward Smith, a banker of Ferriby House, North Ferriby. Smith's Bank was the first multi-provincial bank to be set up outside London in 1658, by Thomas Smith in Nottingham. Further branches were later established in Lincoln, Derby, Gainsborough, Mansfield and Newark.

A London office was established at 1 Lombard Street, in the heart of the banking centre of the City of London. In 1918 it was bought by the National Provincial Bank, which in turn was eventually bought by the National Westminster Bank (Nat West) in 1958. Since 2000, this has been part of the Royal Bank of Scotland group.

Edward Smith's descendants include a Chairman of the Bank of England, and Lord Carrington, the Conservative Foreign Secretary who resigned over the Falklands War in 1982.

Illustrious guests who stayed at the Alexandra Hotel had among them people who played a significant role in national affairs at the time, but, just like any of us in our own families, few might have guessed at how their descendants go on to do even more.

19. OTHER DISTINGUISHED GUESTS, REAL AND IMAGINERY

It is always tempting to speculate and stray from fact to fiction, from possibility to probability, or even simply to start creating and whispering urban myths.

For example, in September 1890 two brothers, nephews of King Kalakana and Queen Kapiolani of Hawaii, came to England to study at the Royal Agricultural College. Prince David Kahelepouli Kawananakoa Pilikoi and Prince Jonah Kuhio Kalanianaole Pilikoi had as their tutor a Yorkshire man who brought them to Bridlington for a break from their studies.

They surprised all the local people by riding the waves on surfboards, and so introduced into this country for the very first time the Hawaiian sport of surfing. They taught their tutor, John Wrightson, how to surf, and while in Bridlington had (it is said) their surfboards cut and shaped (probably from sycamore) by a Bridlington boat builder to their own exact specifications.

On September 22nd 1890, Prince Jonah Kuhio wrote to the Hawaiian Consul, "the weather has been very windy these few days and we like it very much for we like the sea to be rough so that we are able to have surf-riding. We enjoy surf-riding very much and surprise the people to see us riding on the surf."

Unfortunately, there does not appear to be a shred of evidence that the brothers ever stayed at the Alexandra Hotel, although it can only seem highly possible that they at least took some refreshment at what was the very best establishment in the town. What surely cannot be denied is that the hotel guests would have had something to talk about during dinner on that "surf-riding" evening in 1890, and perhaps it is fitting that their visit is celebrated on a plaque fixed to the wall at the southern end of the aptly named "Alexandra Promenade".

Similarly, in 1934 Leading Aircraftsman T. E. Shaw (Lawrence of Arabia) spent the final few winter months of his service life in Bridlington. Lawrence had previously been engaged in an extremely colourful and testing time working for full recognition of the Arab peoples' right of independence during the First World War. He was violently disappointed with the results of the Paris Peace Conference in 1919, which carved up Europe and the Near East among the victorious nations of the First World War, and he withdrew from public life. He subsequently signed up for service in the RAF as Aircraftsman Ross, but when his cover was blown he assumed the name "Shaw". He did not rate Bridlington very highly, describing it rather sourly as an "unfashionable winter resort". He had been stationed in the town previously in 1932-3, and in 1934-5 he was involved in supervising the armour-plating of ten launches to be used for RAF bombing practice. Although vital work, after the deserts of Arabia this can hardly have been an uplifting assignment, and no doubt fuelled his lack of enthusiasm for the town.

He stayed in the Ozone Hotel (now the Royal Yorkshire Yacht Club) near the Spa, and it was on February 26th 1935 that he received his discharge from the RAF at Bridlington and rode off on his bicycle. However, again there is no evidence that this hero of the desert, this bored man who used to ride his motorbike at dangerous speeds along the Promenade, ever ate or drank at the best hotel in town – but it has to be at least possible if not probable?

What is certain is that Vera Brittain stayed in the hotel in 1938. Born in 1873, she was a famous campaigning nurse, feminist and pacifist. Her best-selling book "Testament of Youth", published in 1931, recounted her experiences of the First World War and her journey into pacifism. She died in 1970. From an upper middle class background she was educated at Somerville College, Oxford where she met Winifred Holtby (1898-1935). Holtby had been born at Rudston, near Bridlington, and became a journalist, pamphleteer, socialist and author. Her best-known book "South Riding" is set all around East Yorkshire, and was edited by Brittain and published in 1936. It was made into a successful television series in 1974 and again in 2011. Brittain's own book "Testament of Friendship" (1940) recounted her friendship with Holtby. It was televised in 1979 and made into a film in 2014.

After Vera Brittain married in 1925, Winifred Holtby continued to live with her and helped to raise her children, including the distinguished Labour and later Liberal Democrat Member of Parliament, Shirley Williams who later became Baroness Williams of Crosby.

Later, in the 1950s, when The Alex became also a "home from home" for longer term guests, another famous political name emerges: that of the first Viscount Stansgate, William Wedgewood Benn.

He was a remarkable man and part of a remarkable family. Born in

1877, he was the son of Sir John Benn, a distant relative of Josiah Wedgwood. During the First World War he served in the Royal Flying Corps and was awarded both the DSO and DFC for "exceptional gallantry – a splendid example of courage", having also been awarded the Bronze Medal for Gallantry by the Italian Government. After the war he entered Parliament as a Liberal MP but later crossed the House to join the Labour Party and became Secretary of State for India (1929-31).

In his sixties he returned to the RAF during World War II and rose to the rank of Air Commodore. Aged 67, he was the oldest serving airman flying in bomber air crews and after the war he was appointed Secretary of State for Air (1945-6).

His wife was Margaret Holmes, a forceful and important person in her own right. She was a committed Christian who campaigned for the Ordination of Women to the Anglican Priesthood as early as 1925, decades before others had given much thought to it. The Archbishop of Canterbury pleaded with her to keep quiet – pleas she studiously ignored.

She taught her son, Tony Benn, that the stories of the Bible were about the struggle for justice between God's brave prophets and the powerful kings of Israel who simply wanted to cling to power. In later life, Tony became increasingly agnostic but continued publicly to declare himself a "student of Jesus", and said it was "a great mistake to think the teachings of Jesus outmoded in modern Britain."

Tony Benn himself was a very significant left-wing Labour MP between 1950 and 2000, being the youngest member of the House when first elected. He was a Cabinet Member, serving under Harold Wilson and James Callaghan. He was a chairman of the Labour Party, Secretary of State for Industry, Secretary of State for Energy, and oversaw the opening of the Post Office Tower, the development of Concorde and Nuclear Power. According to his diary entries he was in Bridlington on several occasions in the 1960s on Labour Party business – maybe at the Alexandra Hotel?

His own son Hilary, also a Labour MP, is a considerable orator and served in the Cabinet under both Tony Blair and Gordon Brown, and as Shadow Foreign Secretary. There can have been few more famous twentieth century residents at the Alexandra Hotel than the first Viscount Stansgate, whose family holds the record for three consecutive generations of Cabinet Ministers.

Because the guest-books from the hotel have disappeared, probably destroyed in the fire and demolition that ended the life of the hotel, one of the only other famous names we can be sure about are of a totally different order – the Grumbleweeds! Formed in 1962 and turning professional after success in the television talent show "Opportunity Knocks", they toured the country, appeared often on television and had their own show on BBC Radio 2 in the 1980s. With their zany combination of humour and music they were household names for a time, and stayed at The Alex for a few nights in the 1970s while performing at the Spa. Still touring today, they were playing again at the Spa in July 2018.

What is always pleasant, uplifting and fun is to look back to some of the more famous people who stayed in Bridlington, and at The Alex in particular. Some things, of course, will always remain an enigma.

Ray Purdy remembers one long-term resident of the hotel in its later years who regularly drank in the nearby "Beaconsfield Arms". He is described as resembling the cartoon character "Harris Tweed", who featured on the back page of "The Eagle", the boys' comic of the 1950s and 1960s: rather stout, smartly dressed, with a thin moustache and a monocle. So who was this very distinctive man – does anybody know?

What is wonderful is that history makes no distinction between the comic and the sad, the good and the bad, or the gentle and the traumatic. If we unearth the one we will inevitably discover the other side of human nature, and it is to that we now turn our attention.

20. THE ACID BATH MURDERER

On Thursday 5th July 1934, an apparently innocent entry appeared in the Visitors' Book of the Alexandra Hotel. John George Haigh, aged 35, and Maud Beatrice (Betty) Hamer stayed for the night before being married in Bridlington Registry Office on Friday 6th July.

On the marriage certificate Haigh described himself as a "company director", even though in reality he was a car salesman. Hamer described herself as of "no occupation". But who were these people, and why later did news about Haigh grip the nation?

Haigh was born in Stamford, Lincolnshire, and grew up in the village of Outwood, West Yorkshire. His parents were strict Plymouth Brethren who built a ten foot brick wall around their garden to lock out the evil world beyond. Newspapers, magazines and entertainment of any sort were all forbidden within their enclosed family life.

As a child, he was fond of classical music, won a scholarship first to Queen Elizabeth's Grammar School in Wakefield, and then subsequently another to Wakefield Cathedral where he became a choirboy. But at home Haigh was a lonely child who suffered nightmares. His father told him the blemish on his own head was the result of "sinning as a youth". When such blemishes appeared on Haigh's head too, he became gripped with the thought that he could not get away with anything, and his spiral into evil began as he repeatedly tried to disprove this obsession.

After leaving school he became a motor engineer, then worked in insurance and later in advertising. Aged twenty-one he was made redundant for stealing.

In 1934 he married Betty Hamer at Bridlington Registry Office but the marriage soon disintegrated, and that same year Haigh was imprisoned for fraud. Betty gave birth while he was in prison, but gave up their daughter for adoption and left Haigh. His own family disowned him.

In 1936 he moved to London and worked as a chauffeur to William McSwain, a wealthy owner of amusement arcades, perhaps not dissimilar to those he saw in Bridlington. He then became a self-styled and unlicensed solicitor, and was jailed for a further four years, with more sentences following with regularity for petty criminal activity.

It was while he was in Lincoln prison that he began to plan his "perfect murder", using acid to dissolve the bodies. He experimented on field mice to calculate how long a human body would take to disappear, noting that a mouse dissolved in half an hour.

In 1944 he renewed his association with William McSwain in the Goat Public House in Kensington, London. He was introduced to McSwain's parents, Donald and Amy, who told him about their investments. On 6th September 1944, Haigh hit William on the head with a hammer, dissolved his body in a forty-gallon barrel of acid, and poured the sludge down the drain (claiming later in court he had previously drunk the blood). On 2nd July 1945, he killed Donald and Amy, and disposed of them similarly. He forged documents and claimed their total assets of eight thousand pounds. He then moved into the Onslow Hotel in Kensington, gambling away the whole amount.

In an attempt to solve his lack of money, he then pretended to be interested in buying the home of Dr Archibald Henderson and his wife Rosalie, a couple he had met at the Onslow Hotel. On 12th February 1948 he shot both of them, disposed of them in oil drums filled with acid, sold their assets of eight thousand pounds (again!), but kept their car.

His final victim was Olivia Durand-Deacon, the wealthy widow of solicitor John. They also lived in the Onslow Hotel. He lured her to Crawley, Sussex, shot her in the head, and dissolved her also in acid, but was able to acquire very little money from this murder. But this was his undoing.

The police had begun to become suspicious. They searched his premises in Crawley and found incriminating documents. They then found the drums of acid with three human gallstones and some dentures which the acid could not dissolve, along with some corroded bones and twenty-eight pounds of human fat.

At his trial he confessed to each murder and claimed three more, but these were never substantiated. He pleaded insanity and claimed he had drunk his victims' blood. He said this was all a result of dreams he had as a boy, brainwashed by fanatical over-religious parents, when he saw blood dripping from crucifixes and himself having to drink blood from a cup. He was described as appearing callous, cheerful, bland, and indifferent to his lifestyle.

As he was sentenced to death, he described the judge as looking like "a sheep with its head peering out from under a rhubarb leaf." He was hanged on 10th August 1949, just fifteen years after he had slept in The Alex.

He claimed he believed in reincarnation and would be back to complete his mission. He happily allowed Madame Tussaud's Waxworks to take a mould and make a death-mask. The newspapers and cinema newsreels were full of the lurid details, calling him the "acid bath vampire", and a number of books have been written recounting the story.

In 1951, his case was dramatized on BBC radio as "The Jar of Acid" in the series "The Black Museum". In 2002 Martin Clunes brilliantly and chillingly played Haigh in the ITV drama "A is for Acid", (now available on DVD), and in 2011 Nigel Fairs played Haigh in the audio-drama "In Conversation with an Acid Bath Murderer".

Madame Tussaud's exhibited his wax effigy for some years, and he appeared as a vision in episode three, season twelve, of the television series "Bones". Two heavy metal bands, Macabre and Church of Misery, have recorded songs about him.

The staff who booked him in at the Alexandra Hotel in 1934, the fellow guests in adjacent rooms, and those near him at breakfast, can all have had no idea how close they came to being pulled into his terrible story. And of course, that raises a very personal question for all of us. In the 1930s, the Alexandra Hotel was a very respectable place to stay. So the last time you stayed in a hotel, did you wonder who might have slept in your bed the night before you arrived?

Reading about one night in a now-disappeared hotel, on the northeast coast in 1934, can suddenly seem very immediate, wherever we are and whatever the date!

BRIDLINGTON.
"The King of Watering Places."

The Alexandra Hotel,

The finest and most up-to-date Hotel on the East Coast.
Open all the year round.

SPECIAL ATTRACTION FOR EASTER:
ORCHESTRA. JAZZ TEAS. DANCING EVERY EVENING. BILLIARDS. BRIDGE. &C., &C.

Where to motor for a good Lunch or Dinner.
Wines and Spirits of the very best.

Tel. 1 Bridlington.
Tel. Address: "Alexandra Hotel."

For Tariff, apply
MISS WEBSTER, Manageress

An advertisement from 1920 features a very upmarket and trend-setting novelty, "Jazz Teas" in the hotel, and describes Bridlington as "The King of Watering Places".

Alexandra Hotel,
BRIDLINGTON.

Telegrams—"ALEXANDRA HOTEL, BRIDLINGTON."
Telephone—2254.

RE-DECORATED IN ENTIRETY.

THE LEADING HOTEL
IN BRIDLINGTON.

Unsurpassed Situation overlooking Bay, Flamborough Head and Private Grounds.

Nine Hole Miniature Golf Course.   Dancing.

FULLY LICENSED.
LIFT.

Open all the year round.   Heated throughout.

This advertisement boasts a nine-hole mini golf course as a major attraction, together with "heating throughout!"

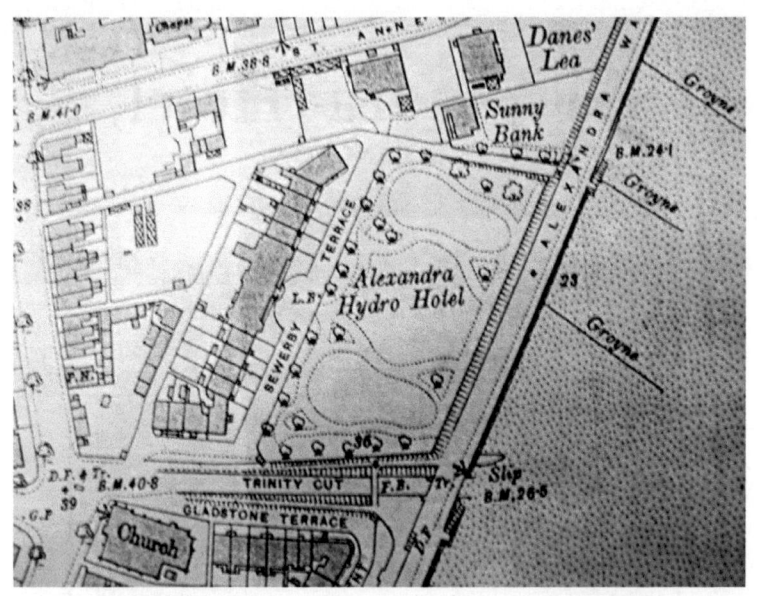

A map of 1911 shows the Hydro Hotel with landscaped gardens and paths.

By 1928, a street map shows the landscaped gardens still intact, but it is no longer a "hydro" hotel.

The paths of the gardens offered a leisurely walk while taking the air.

The meandering paths and flower-beds made a pleasant location
for sharing gossip or agreeing business deals.

View of the Grounds and Sea taken from the Hydro.

The full extent of the curving paths can be seen from a hotel balcony.

The winding paths helped a little exercise before the evening meal.

The statue of Pandora stands as a point of interest in the gardens, 1910.

Pandora is watched over by the hotel, proudly flying flags on the front corners of each turret.

The statue of Pandora which once stood in the gardens of the hotel is probably the one which now stands in the Rose Garden of Sewerby Hall.

The front gardens, having become tennis courts.

The tennis courts of the front gardens, to the left of the path.

An aerial photograph showing pitch and putt on the front lawns in 1928.

An aerial photograph of the front lawns in 1947.

The front gardens as simplified lawns in the 1960s.

Trinity Cut c. 1930 and the Alexandra Hotel.
A view of the hotel from Trinity Cut in 1930.

A lifeboat being launched from Trinity Cut would always be a source of excitement for hotel guests. This one, the second to be named the "George and Jane Walker," was in use between 1899 and 1931. People seem too well-dressed for this to have been a rushed launch to a vessel in distress, and there appears to be no wind. It is probably a ceremonial launch after a Lifeboat Guild garden party on the hotel lawns.

The lifeboat "George and Jane Walker" hauled by horses, being launched from Trinity Cut, and dated between 1905 and 1910, again probably after a garden party on the hotel lawns.

The lifeboat "The Tillie Morrison Sheffield II" (1953 – 1967) being launched from Trinity Cut at the end of the Lifeboat Guild garden party in 1956. On the right is Head Launcher, Geoff Haggard.

A ceremonial lifeboat launch involving lots of onlookers.

A small rowing boat could always be pulled out to sea by the strong currents and tides, needing a rescue by the lifeboat. Note the canvas changing tents on the beach in front of the hotel.

Bathing machines line up in front of the hotel, ready to be used by guests.

Bathing huts were stored in Trinity Cut when not in use.

In Trinity Cut bathing machines line up ready for use.

Bathing machines on North Beach from George Walker's "The Costume of Yorkshire" (1814).

The perils of the sea were not to be underestimated
when using bathing machines.

Despite modest bathing suits and bathing machines, open flirting was not uncommon for the benefit of the men on the beach with telescopes!

A humorous reflection on the women paid to assist those using bathing machines.

Collectable Goss China ornaments were popular in the early twentieth century. This example is of a Bridlington bathing machine.

Bridlington's coat of arms on the Goss China bathing machine.

The Goss China Bridlington bathing machine encourages
an early morning dip before breakfast!

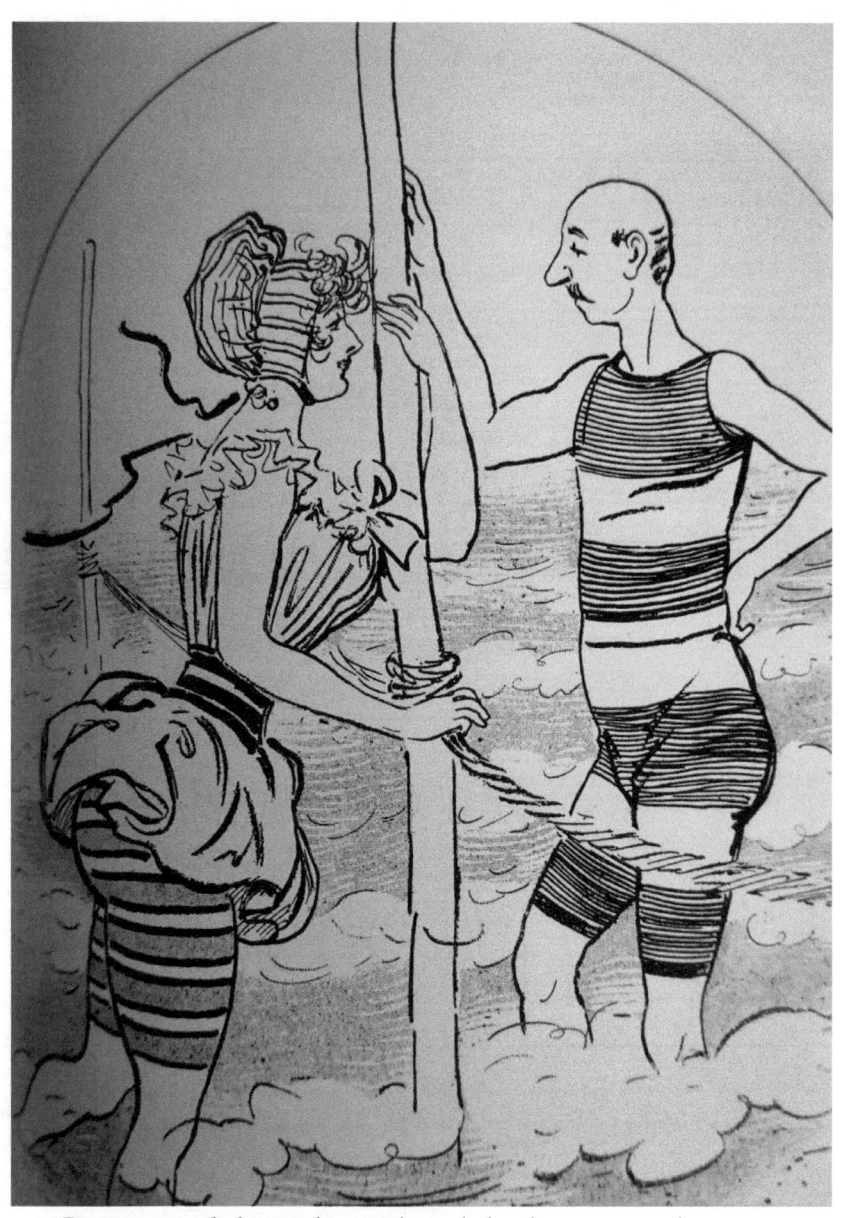

Rope suspended on poles was intended to keep men and women separated but, of course, was never effective.

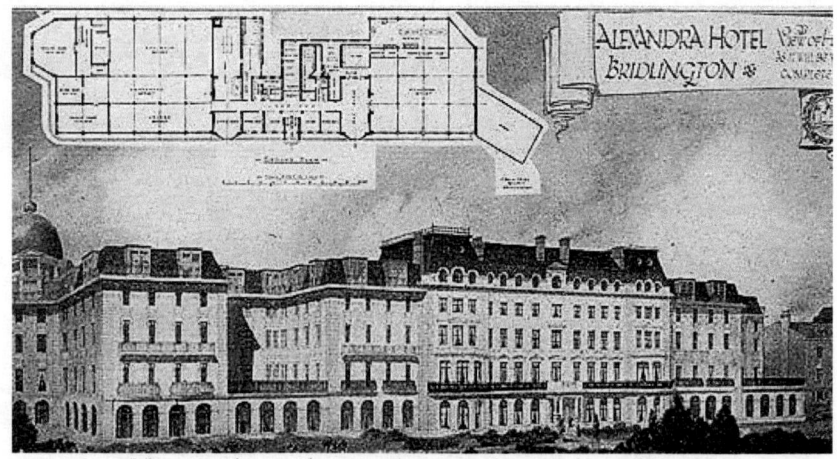

The massive and ornate proposed extension of 1920,
which was never built.

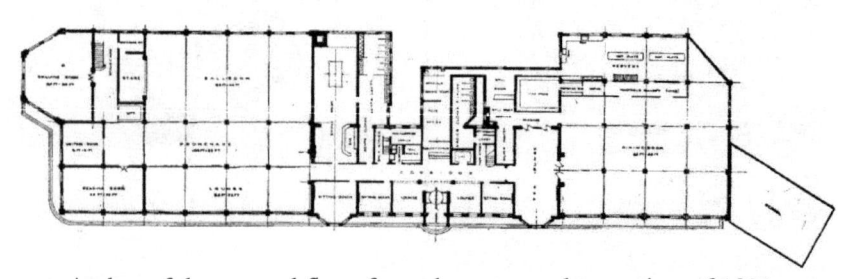

A plan of the ground floor from the proposed extension of 1920,
even showing a school room to the right.

The Floral Hall, built by Percy Newbound in 1920, owner of the hotel.

A fire destroyed the Floral Hall in 1923, hours before the famous George Robey was to perform there.

BRIDLINGTON

Plan and Particulars
OF
THE VALUABLE
FREEHOLD ESTATE
KNOWN AS
"THE ALEXANDRA HOTEL"
together with the whole of the
EXCELLENT FURNITURE
FIXTURES and FITTINGS
as a going concern
AND WHICH

Messrs. HEPPER & SONS

WILL
SELL BY AUCTION
IN THEIR
Estate Sale Room, East Parade, Leeds
ON
TUESDAY, 8th JULY 1924
at 3 o'clock precisely

Subject to the General Conditions of Sale of the Yorkshire Union of Law Societies and to Special Conditions to be produced at the time of Sale.

Copies hereof and further information may be had from the undermentioned—

HEPPER & SONS	H. J. S. WOODHOUSE & CO.
Auctioneers East Parade	*Solicitors* 11 Clarges Street, Mayfair
LEEDS	LONDON W.1.

SCATCHERD, HOPKINS & BRIGHOUSE
Solicitors 20 Park Row, LEEDS

The auction papers of 8th July 1924.

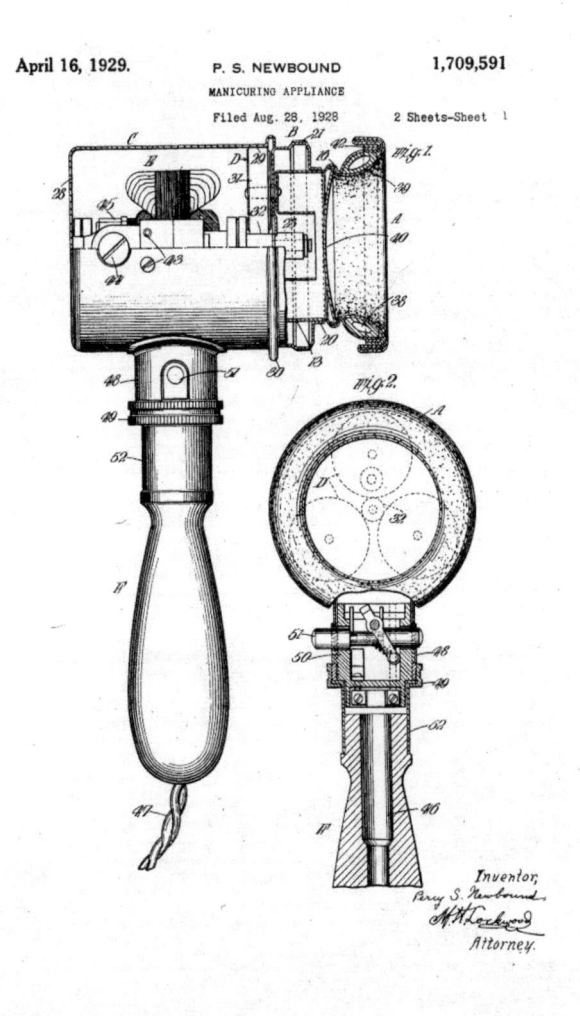

Diagram of hotel owner Percy Newbound's 1928 patent
"Motor Driven Polishing Device for Nails."

167

Some adjacent houses were demolished to make way
for the ground floor extensions to be built.

In the foreground, preparations are made for an event on the front lawn, and in the background is the framework for the new ground floor extensions on each side.

The new ground floor extensions are in place, and the hotel proudly flies its own flag.

Thomas Wilson, the shipping magnate who stayed at the hotel as an early guest.

TRANBY CROFT.
Sep 11, 1890.

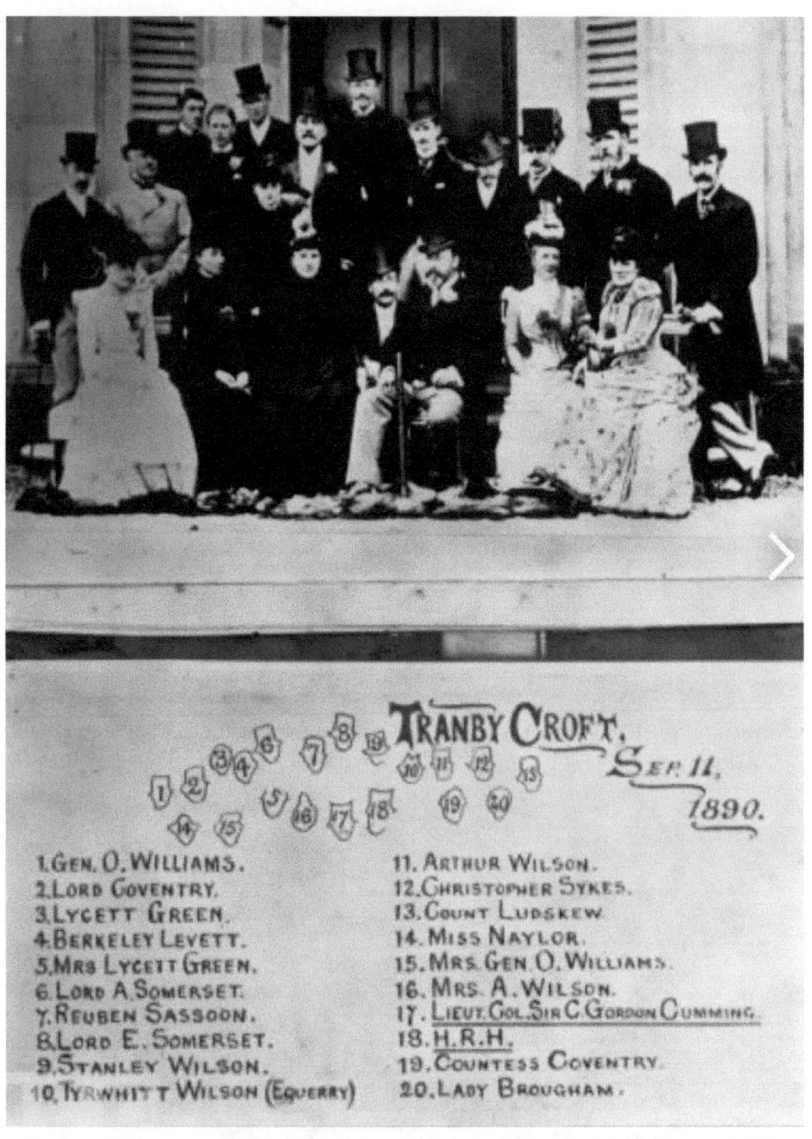

1. Gen. O. Williams.
2. Lord Coventry.
3. Lycett Green.
4. Berkeley Levett.
5. Mrs Lycett Green.
6. Lord A. Somerset.
7. Reuben Sassoon.
8. Lord E. Somerset.
9. Stanley Wilson.
10. Tyrwhitt Wilson (Equerry)
11. Arthur Wilson.
12. Christopher Sykes.
13. Count Ludskew.
14. Miss Naylor.
15. Mrs. Gen. O. Williams.
16. Mrs. A. Wilson.
17. Lieut. Col. Sir C Gordon Cumming.
18. H.R.H.
19. Countess Coventry.
20. Lady Brougham.

Arthur Wilson stayed at The Alex with his father in 1868, but in 1890 hosted an illegal gambling party at the family home. With guests including the Prince of Wales, and accusations of cheating, a very public court case followed and a national scandal rocked the monarchy.

> UNITED COMMERCIAL TRAVELLERS' ASSOCIATION
> OF GREAT BRITAIN AND IRELAND.
>
> (U.K.C.T.A.)   INCORPORATED
>
> BRIDLINGTON, DRIFFIELD AND DISTRICT BRANCH.
> NEW YEAR'S EVE
> # DINNER-DANCE
> IN AID OF COMMERCIAL TRAVELLERS CHARITIES.
> WILL BE HELD AT THE
> ALEXANDRA HOTEL,
> BRIDLINGTON.
> ON TUESDAY, DECEMBER 31ST., 1929.
> DINNER 8 p.m.   CARRIAGES 2 a.m.
> AUGMENTED DANCE BAND.
> TICKETS 8/6 EACH (Inclusive)
> Right of Admission Reserved.

An invitation to a New Year's Eve charity dinner-dance organised by the local branch of The United Commercial Travellers' Association, 1929.

The advent of the motor car made a huge difference to the type of guests who could come for a holiday at the hotel.

John Haigh, the "Acid Bath Murderer", who stayed at the hotel in 1934.

One of the many books
written about John Haigh.

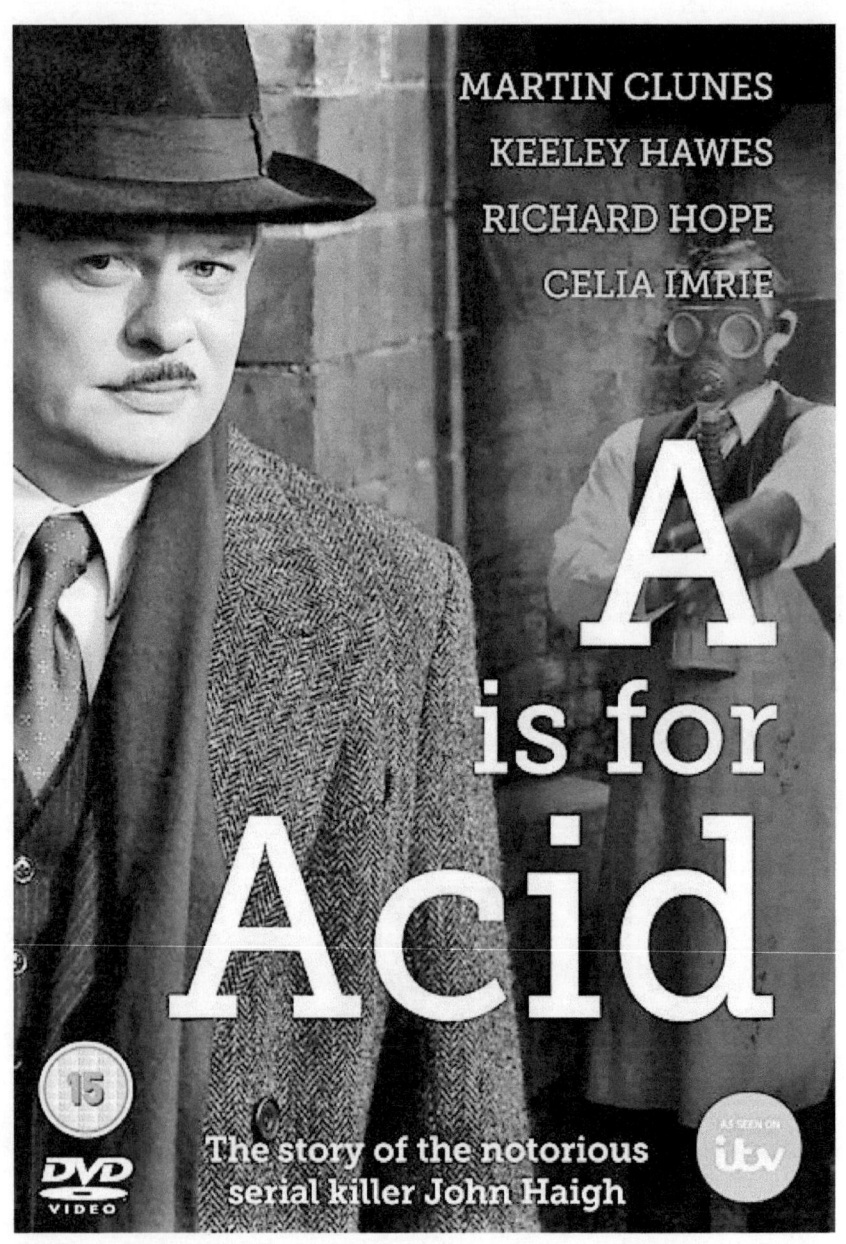

ITV produced a film about John Haigh in 2002, starring Martin Clunes.

The Hawaiian Princes who introduced surfing while at Bridlington in 1890.

T. E. Lawrence (Lawrence of Arabia) stationed in Bridlington between 1925 and 1935.

Vera Brittain, the ardent pacifist and socialist, who stayed at the hotel in 1938.

William Wedgewood-Benn, The First Viscount Stansgate,
a resident of the hotel in the 1950s.

Sir Anthony Wedgewood-Benn, later known as Tony Benn after renouncing his peerage.

The 1960s pop star Adam Faith opening the 1963 garden party of the Ladies' Lifeboat Association on the front lawn of the hotel.

Adam Faith judging a beauty pageant on Bridlington's South Beach in 1963.

The comedic pop group, The Grumbleweeds, stayed at the hotel in the 1960s.

The Barron Knights played at the hotel in the 1970s.

(iv) TEAMS AND DREAMS

21. BELOW STAIRS

One of the great injustices of life is that those people who are vital to the wellbeing of society are often the least recognised, most unknown, and lowest paid.

In any organisation, it is obvious that good management at the top is vital, whether it is the chief executive, the managing director, the Prime Minister or the head teacher. Yet when we ask: who is the one person who can get a hospital closed overnight, the answer is the cleaner. Without good cleaners, disease and infections spread and the hospital will cease to function. In the supermarket, it is the junior sales assistant with a cheery or a grumpy disposition who can encourage a customer to return or never set foot in there again.

Similarly, in a hotel, if the food is not cooked and served well, if the rooms are not clean, if the heating is inadequate, if the gardens are overgrown, then guests simply will not return, bookings will plummet, and decline and closure will become real possibilities.

It is therefore a great pity that, when playing detective and trying to piece together the story of The Alex, there are all sorts of records about the rich who invested their fortunes in the hotel, famous people associated with it, notorious guests who stayed there, yet very little about the very people without whom it could never have functioned – the staff, those "below stairs".

Until very recently, historians tended to be people from the upper or leisured classes who wrote about their own kind. Biographies abound about military and political leaders, great inventors and engineers, explorers and social activists. When Charles Dickens wrote "Oliver Twist" about the life in the workhouse, and Charles Kingsley wrote "The Water Babies" about the appalling conditions of working children, they broke the mould. Indeed, Charles Dickens wrote a particularly relevant and perceptive observation while watching children on the beach in his own seaside home town of Broadstairs in Kent: "The sands are the children's greatest resort. They cluster there, like ants: so busy burying their particular friends, and making castles with infinite labour which the next tide overthrows, that it is curious to consider how their play, to the music of the sea, foreshadows the reality of their after lives." The observations which informed his works, and the subsequent impact of Dickens and his contemporary campaigners for a better world cannot be overestimated.

So what do we know about the staff at the Alexandra Hotel? In the early days, we have little more than the records of census returns, but they are still revealing:

1871

NAME	AGE	RANK	BORN
Edwin Taylor	48	Hotel Keeper	Bridlington
Margaret Taylor	49	Wife	Bridlington
Margaret Spence	11	Daughter	Filey
Francis James Taylor	11	Son, scholar	Hull
Gertrude Taylor	11	Daughter, scholar	Filey
Elizabeth Taylor	6	Daughter, scholar	Hull

Harry Alexander Taylor	4	Son	Bridlington
James Jameson	48	Vintner/merchant	Cottingham
Jane Jameson	42	Wife	Cottingham
Margaret Clayton	23	Unmarried/governess	St Ives, Cambs
Selina Rooks	40	Nurse	Rusteston (Rudston?)
Mary Smith	36	Cook	Yorkshire
Amelia Waite	30	Widow/kitchen maid	Yorkshire
Anne Chambers	25	Unmarried/housemaid	Yorkshire
Jane Garlin	19	Unmarried/barmaid	Yorkshire
John Lamplugh	22	Porter	Yorkshire
Octavia Danby	16	Unmarried/housemaid	Yorkshire
Mary Anne Topple	17	Unmarried/housemaid	Yorkshire

So in 1871, while the hotel was in its infancy we see a husband and wife in charge of the hotel, and who lived in with their family, but there are unanswered questions here. First, Edwin Taylor describes himself as "Hotel Keeper". An advertisement of 1872 calls the hotel "Taylor's Alexandra Hotel". Surviving examples of early hotel crockery have a crest with the words "Taylor's" and "Alexandra Hotel". These would suggest Edwin Taylor was the owner rather than just the keeper, or at least the legal lessee of the business. What exactly was his relationship with the hotel? He was certainly very young to have owned such a business, but perhaps he had family money?

Second, he is no longer the "hotel keeper" by 1881. In Bridlington

Cemetery there is a headstone marking the grave of Margaret Taylor of Bridlington Quay, who died in 1873 aged 43. She is described as the wife of Edwin Taylor. Yet in the 1871 Census she is recorded as aged 49. It seems unlikely that there would be two Edwin and Margaret Taylors, and it just might be that the most likely explanation is that the Census record is unwittingly wrong, not an uncommon occurrence.

If this Margaret and Edwin Taylor were the ones managing the hotel, then the death of Margaret could explain why Edwin decided to move away, perhaps emotionally or physically unable to continue this demanding work and bring up his family.

In that 1871 Census, there are some (not many) guests who decided to enter the hotel as their abode for that night, rather than their own home (unless they really did live full-time in the hotel), and then a number of staff.

It would appear there were seven staff who lived in the hotel and presumably had their wages reduced accordingly. However, for a hotel of this size, there must have been a lot more staff involved, and it may have been that they were people who lived locally at home, but came in to work each day.

In any hotel of substance there was a definite order of precedence:

Manager: the steward of the place, responsible for standards and good financial management, often aided by a sub-manager.
Housekeeper: responsible for the female staff in particular, and also probably for the cellar man and laundry staff.
Cook/Chef: in charge of all the meals and the staff in the kitchen.

	Long hours and hot conditions would have been the norm, and an eye for detail essential. There may be under-chefs for each of meat, fish, vegetables, pastries, cold meats and desserts.
Porters:	The Head Porter would be in charge of the Day Porters and the Night Porters who would lift heavy luggage from carriages to the rooms and be general-purpose workers.
Waiters	A Head Waiter would have under him staff each responsible for different rooms.
Maids	In the Alexandra Hotel with its hundred or so fireplaces, each fire had to be made and tended daily, fireplaces cleaned, coal lifted upstairs constantly – and all, looking at the census, by relatively young women who were registered as housemaids.
Others	the lift attendants and Receptionist all had their important place too. Cleaners, gardeners and nannies to care for guests' children (especially at meal times when they would eat separately) were all vital people in the team.

The governess and nurse mentioned in this 1871 census may have been part of the hotel staff available for guests, or may have been personal to the manager's family, or may even have been personal to the guests, Mr and Mrs Jameson. We shall never know. However, whatever the case here, they would have been valued and trusted people on fairly intimate terms with their employer.

There would also have been kitchen maids, scullery maids, laundry maids, gardeners and so on, but again of these we know nothing –

their names, ages, level of pay or conditions of employment are all lost in the mists of time.

This was an era when workers had few rights, could be hired and fired at will, where pay scales were subject to no regulations, hours were long, work was exhausting, and abuse by guests and management would be normal. There was no sick-pay, maternity leave, pension, and little free time for entertainment. Pregnancy resulted in dismissal, and rural girls who came into the town for work were particularly vulnerable to being pestered by suitors. Some probably had run away from home and so were especially at risk.

Good manners were expected in public. Staff would be instructed: do not fidget when being addressed; only speak when spoken to; always speak quietly and address guests as "sir" or "madam"; never offer your opinion on anything; always stand back to let other pass; be punctual for everything through the day; friends and relatives may not be received into the building without permission; all breakages would be deducted from the meagre wages; and so it goes on. Life was strictly regulated and hard, but for many it was paid work in times when the alternatives could be a lot worse.

For those living-in, the attic floor of the hotel housed the staff bedrooms. The cook would probably have had a room of her own, and the maids probably shared rooms, often with more privacy and comfort than they had enjoyed at home. There would have been a sense of camaraderie and mutual care in amongst the inevitable squabbles, petty pilfering and gossip.

This Census of 1871 revealed that, across the nation, fifteen per cent of the population were in service, either in domestic houses or in the hospitality trade of hotels and restaurants.

When we move on ten years we find the names have all changed in this census return:

1881

NAME	AGE	RANK	BORN
Cyril Wright	35	Hotel-keeper	Sevenoaks, Kent
Margaret Wright	28	Wife	Holloway, London
Emma Foster	18	Unmarried/niece	Holloway, London
Jane Thompson	42	Widow/cook	Gainsborough
Fanny Hichling	34	Widow/chambermaid	Australia
Elizabeth Brown	19	Unmarried/housemaid	Bridlington
John Musgrove	35	Visitor/MA Cambridge	Armsley
Sidney Williamson	19	Visitor/student of music	Shipton

Here we find a new "hotel keeper", Cyril Wright, and fewer live-in staff, with presumably more living at home in town. Again, there must have been many more staff about whom we know nothing.

The change of names is evident again ten years later:

1891

NAME	AGE	RANK	BORN
Mary Burneston	52	Widow/Hotel Keeper	Leeds

Clara Burneston	26	Daughter	Leeds
Charles Curtis	52	Married, partner and hotel-keeper, auctioneer	Leeds
Mary Curtis	50	Wife	Wormsley
James Dalziel	27	Book-keeper	Scotland
Ann Murgatroyd	54	Widow/cook	Roehampton
Hannah Appleby	25	Unmarried/housemaid	Seamer
Charlotte Fowhill	25	Unmarried/housemaid	Bempton
Maud Freer	18	Unmarried/seamstress	Seamer
Emily Hornby	18	Unmarried/housemaid	Driffield
Charles Walker	22	Domestic servant	Leeds
Herman Sommer	19	Waiter	Holstein
Henry Freer	19	Carpet Maker	Scarborough

Again, we see a different "hotel keeper," Mary Burneston, significantly a woman this time, who assumed responsibility with Charles Curtis. He obviously diversified his interests and describes himself as "partner, hotel keeper and auctioneer". For the first time we have evidence of a member of staff from overseas: Herman Sommer, a waiter, born in Holstein, Germany – an early example of a migrant worker from Europe?

This national Census of 1891 revealed that nationally, now one and a third million girls and women worked in domestic service of some description.

A further ten years later and the same management is in place, although Charles Curtis now describes his various entrepreneurial activities differently, suggesting he is doing rather well:

1901

NAME	AGE	RANK	BORN
Charles Curtis	62	Employer, Local Sheriff's Officer, Director and Manager	York
Mary Curtis	60	Wife	Wormsley
Mary Burniston	62	Manager/Director	Leeds
Clara Burniston	36	Unmarried	Leeds
John Mercer	47	Servant	Sproatley
? Murgatroyd	20	Unmarried/servant	Leeds
Margaret Bayram	24	Unmarried/servant	Doncaster
Charles Disparo	16	Servant	York
Rebecca Major	27	Servant	North Barton

The next census suggests again few staff actually live in the hotel, and perhaps this is an indication that Bridlington as a town has grown and more staff are available locally, but we have no certainty:

1911

NAME	AGE	RANK	BORN
Mary Roberts	46	Manageress	Bray, Ireland
Edward Hallingworth	91	Boarder/employer	Yorkshire
? Greene	28	Boarder	Bastable
Sarah Rees	20	Lady's Maid	Merthyr Tydfil
Sophie	24	Book keeper	Yorkshire

Tanieman			
Helena Smealey	23	Housemaid	Nottingham
Alfred Radley	24	Waiter	Brighton
Pelay Mays	19	Porter	York
Sophia Muckle	18	Servant	Hull
Mary ?	28	Housekeeper	Ireland
Emily Roberts	34	Visitor	Bray, Ireland

So the lists go on. Frustratingly, we know nothing about most of these people without the benefit of tracing the genealogy of each of them. But even that would probably not reveal why particular staff were attracted to Bridlington, how long they stayed, or how they behaved. We have no idea if they left of their own accord or were sacked, or of the conditions under which they worked.

This is such a pity, for each of these early staff members would have been under the constant scrutiny of their employers. Those who met guests may have been either highly valued or scarcely noticed. Stories about them and between them must surely have abounded as gossip is the lifeblood of all organisations.

As late as the 1970s Jayne Atkinson worked as a waitress in The Alex for a few months. It was one of the permanent guests, an elderly gentleman in his seventies, who took the time to teach her to be a "silver service waitress". That suggests a kindly and relaxed relationship between staff and guests, but as for the early days, the stories of the staff have disappeared along with the bricks and the mortar. Yet the people of these stories will always be the real heroes of The Alex: the unsung heroes of Bridlington's great history of generous hospitality.

22. THE HATJE DYNASTY

Bridlington has a proud record of welcoming people not only as tourists and holidaymakers, but also as new residents and as part of the workforce contributing to the local economy. Today, a considerable number of the local community are people who have pleasant memories of holidays in the town, and who eventually came to retire by the seaside.

In the 1930s, a family arrived from Scotland, where they had already had good experience of running hotels. William Hatje, whose family was originally from Germany, was born in Hamburg in 1872, and arrived in Scotland as a young man. We have no idea what led him to make this great adventure, but it is intriguing to note that in the 1901 Census his was the only "Hatje" registration in the United Kingdom, whereas there were many in America registered between 1880 and 1920, with catering (surely no coincidence) listed as a predominant trade or profession.

He had married Isabella Gordon Mornoch, born in 1875, in Aberdeen. Their first hotel was The Grand Hotel in Lerwick in the Shetlands, where all their children were born and baptised in the hotel itself! The Minister was brought to the hotel rather than everyone going to the nearest Kirk, and the children were all baptised in pairs (for ease and economy?), except their fifth child, Vaila, who was named after one of the smaller Shetland islands. An enterprising and hardworking couple, they often owned two hotels at the same time, and when they bought The Alex, they also acquired a hotel in Lowestoft.

Isabella, known by everyone as "The Duchess", was very firm and precise and ran the staff of the hotel with strict discipline and an eye for detail. For example, she would serve the children of guests with a sandwich high-tea at 4.30pm, so that the adults could enjoy their evening meal in peace. Then at 6.25pm precisely she would enter the dining room to inspect the tables, check that the cutlery, crockery, serviettes and glasses were all set immaculately, straighten every table cloth, and then at exactly 6.30pm she would bang the gong to call the guests to dinner. Clearly, here was someone determined to maintain the high standards expected of a Victorian grand hotel, and so retain a good calibre of guests willing to pay good money to enjoy traditional hospitality.

The family lived at conveniently neighbouring 5 Lamplugh Road which is where Isabella continued to live after her husband died in 1938, and until her youngest son Walter married Kathleen Robinson in 1955. At that point, Isabella moved into the hotel and her middle son, Norman, lived nearby with his family in Lamplugh Square. They retained private quarters in the hotel itself to ensure there was always someone on duty, both day and night. The family rooms in the hotel were reached by turning right at the top of the main stairs on the first floor, and passing through double doors with net curtains covering the glazed windows.

In these hallowed rooms, naturally out of bounds to guests, were a drawing room and two single bedrooms. When Mr and Mrs Hatje retired from actively running the hotel, their sons Walter and Norman became directors and managed The Alex, sleeping in these single bedrooms while on overnight duty. Their older brother, Bill (described as rather eccentric!) also had a room there. These rooms had beautiful views of the bay through the large windows, looking over the lawns with their croquet and pitch and putt games. Their bathroom was suitably imposing: a green onyx suite which included a bath so large it needed two steps up to it.

A lot of formal dinners were held in the dining room beneath the owners' quarters, and these ranged from dinner dances organised by the Society of Licensed Victuallers, the Caledonian Society, the Royal Yorkshire Yacht Club, and Scottish dancing classes were held there weekly (by Mr & Mrs Hatje from Scotland themselves?). This is in addition to the countless number of wedding receptions and private functions.

All this required a considerable staff who themselves needed to be trusted to do their job well, to work as a team, and to accept being managed by owners who knew exactly what they wanted. There is one particular example of how those working at The Alex responded calmly and efficiently to potential disasters. In August 1936, a fire broke out in the attic. Such was the self-control of the whole team that the guests all continued to enjoy their evening meal, completely unaware that firemen were at work at high level behind the hotel, extinguishing the blaze. What an amazing testimony to careful leadership by the management and good discipline among the whole staff!

Sarah Davidson, who has kindly provided this snapshot of life at the hotel, is a granddaughter of William and Isabella Hatje, and remembers with affection some of the key staff: Miss Sharpe (the receptionist who would give children sweets), Mrs Boffee (who worked in the office), Marjorie (the housekeeper/head chambermaid), Aldo (the Italian head waiter), and Johnny the cocktail waiter who, judging by the comments posted on Facebook and recorded in another chapter, made a considerable impression on so many guests – to be remembered fondly fifty years later by so many is no mean feat!

A headstone in Bridlington Cemetery records that William Hatje died on 19th April 1938 aged 63, and his wife Isabella died eighteen years later on 18th May 1956, aged 81. Their sons, Walter and Norman (of whom more later), continued to run the hotel successfully, and finally sold it in 1964 to Mr Tiffany (who then sold it on to Mr Crocker). By this time the era of package holidays abroad was beginning to take hold, and the two sons could see the future of grand hotels in Britain's seaside resorts was far from certain.

For those who like conspiracy theories and are intrigued by mysteries and rumours, it was in 1963 that Adam Faith was the headline act at the Spa for the summer season and opened a garden party on the lawns of the hotel. It was common knowledge that he liked the town and had formed a number of very close friendships with local people. It was rumoured that this pop star, who later became famous also as an adventurous businessman and investor, helped to fund the purchase of the hotel by Mr Tiffany. Shrouded in the clouds of hidden history, the true facts have probably completely disappeared from public view as surely as has the hotel itself – but it is intriguing to wonder, and we do love gossip.

23. JOLLY HARD WORK!

The warm glow of nostalgia is always an easy frame of mind into which we can retreat: nice hot summers, time to relax, a simpler lifestyle, less stress, fewer complications, and easier decisions. Of course, managing a hotel as a financial success never was like that, and certainly did not seem like that at the time.

Fashion is always fickle, and can change with little warning. This is certainly true in the hotel trade, and makes the business of serving the public both precarious and exhausting. We can indulge in fanciful stories about the staff: the obsequious waiter, the eagle-eyed manager, the portly chef, or the careless porter. We can tell stories about the guests – the gruff retired colonel, the devious little children, and the kindly old couple. But the real heroes and villains of the stories are always the hotels themselves, built to make a fortune for their founders and risking huge sums of money for investors. Today's hotels may have push-button controls, white faux-leather, shiny chrome and LED lights, but the business is the same now as it was when The Alex was built: that of selling a product – hospitality. In the end, it is hard economics that govern everything, and this was always so for The Alex from its birth to its demise.

The Alexandra Hotel was built in 1866. Just eleven years later a national newspaper, the Daily Star, carried the observation: "Forty years ago it was almost a sign of eccentricity to put up a hotel," and then went on to write about the frenzy of energy across the country to build grand hotels for a new class of holidaymakers. The old coaching inns along routes like the Great North Road (the A1) which provided mediocre rooms and poor meals for travellers while the coaching horses were changed, were giving way to new hotels in towns, cities, and emerging resorts. These new hotels were built not for a single-night stopover, but as a comfortable destination in itself – a place to stay, relax and entertain friends and business colleagues. London saw huge enterprises like The Clarendon and Pulteney's where the wealthy stayed. Near Victoria Station the Grosvenor Hotel built in 1858 looked like a large forerunner of The Alex: four turrets, a pavilion roof, and windows becoming smaller with each of its six floors – all with the novelty of a "rising room", a fancy name for a lift. In Buxton's Royal Crescent three large hotels (The Grand, The Centre and St Anne's) emerged to serve this inland freshwater spa town before seawater became the fashion. The Southport Palace opened in 1866 and the Cavendish Hotel in Eastbourne in 1873. Often these were run by managers employed by the owners. Where documented history lets us down with The Alex is being able to know quite if, when, and how ownership and on-site management became divorced and re-united.

The effect of the rise in the number of travellers cannot be overestimated. In 1833 alone coach and rail passengers nationally numbered about two and a half million. It was seen as an economic bonanza waiting to be grasped with both hands. In a reaction to the stricter rules of eighteenth century architecture, new money could be lavished on ornate extravagance. Classical pillars and the straight line of Georgian crescents gave way to highly decorative Italian, French and Gothic influences. The influential architect A. W. N. Pugin wanted "Christian architecture" reflecting continental Catholicism to replace the pagan influence of Greek and Roman secularism. When plans were submitted for the Alexandra Hotel, the directors (including two churchwardens of Bridlington Priory) were obviously swept along in this. But it all added to the cost.

Architects, planners and investors all exuded an aura of self-assured, enthusiastic, dynamic, God-fearing confidence. Just like the Alexandra Hotel, similar designs were also seen around the coast at Brighton, Bournemouth, Margate, and closer to home at Scarborough.

Built a year later than the Alexandra Hotel, The Grand in Scarborough cost one hundred thousand pounds (about twelve million pounds today). It was even larger and more ostentatious than The Alex with its four towers, twelve floors, fifty-two chimneys and three hundred and sixty-five bedrooms (all reflecting numbers in the calendar year), and designed for ever to link it closely to royalty, being built in the shape of a "V" to honour Queen Victoria. What is remarkable is that after being hit by thirty shells during the First World War, it cost a further hundred thousand pounds to renovate. The continual ongoing costs were astonishing, and eventually it was bought by Butlins in 1978 and then by the Britannia Group in 2004, which two years later spent seven million pounds refurbishing it. Now a Grade Two Listed Historic Building it is still greedy for cash. Although the Alexandra Hotel was a smaller enterprise, it was built at the same time and in a similar style, and the parallels for demanding huge sums of money for costly upkeep are obvious.

The new Stock Companies Act of 1844 had made it initially much easier to issue shares and raise capital for all sorts of business ventures (including the Alexandra Hotel), and nationally over one hundred and twenty million pounds was raised each year in each of the first fifty years, including for hotel premises. It was not always safe or straightforward. The Langham Hotel in Portland Place, London, was costed at one hundred and fifty thousand pounds in 1862, but eventually cost an extra thirty thousand pounds to build. These were vast amount of money, and it is quite probable that investors everywhere, in the midst of their excitement, also experienced considerable stress, anxiety and sleepless nights – including in Bridlington!

Once built, running costs were also frightening. In 1870 the Grand Pump Room Hotel in Bath cost six thousand pounds per year to run, of which only eight hundred and ninety five pounds was staff wages. Cutlery cost three thousand six hundred pounds, carriages three hundred and sixteen pounds, laundry two hundred and twenty-seven pounds, coal and gas three hundred pounds and advertising two hundred pounds.

As far as returns for the investors are concerned, the Pump Room Hotel paid a dividend of two hundred pounds and the Queens Hotel in Hastings paid a fifteen per cent return in 1862. But the Grand Hotel in Scarborough, which originally only opened for July and August each year, not enjoying the temperate climate of places like Torquay and Bournemouth, only paid three and a half per cent in 1877, nil in 1878, and one per cent in 1879. Frustratingly, the figures for the Alexandra Hotel are not known, but these other similar hotels demonstrate the risky venture the hotel trade has always been.

The wages bill may not have been a large part of the annual expenditure, but the management of all the people employed was always a major concern. Again, the total number employed at The Alex has been lost, but figures at similar establishments are revealing. A typical annual salary in 1883 might have been sixty pounds for a cook, fifty pounds for a head waiter, thirty-six pounds for a cellar man, twenty-four pounds for a head porter or laundress or a head chambermaid. Wages were typically ten per cent of the running costs. All this was on top of the cost of accommodating some of the staff in the attic-floor. Men's and women's rooms and dormitories were usually approached by separate staircases to prevent any romances (always a nuisance to the management!), and life was very hierarchical with what might seem like double standards. For example, for a member of staff to expect a tip was actively discouraged, and yet the manager of the Victoria Hotel, Southport, was given a bonus of ninety-six pounds in 1885.

With all these high overheads and seasonal uncertainties, hotel failures were not uncommon. Hatchetts Hotel in Piccadilly was built in 1886 for one hundred and twenty thousand pounds, but was sold for half that amount just one year later. The Northumberland Avenue Hotel in London asked investors for two hundred thousand pounds, but construction costs eventually came in at five hundred and twenty thousand pounds. It opened in 1887, but its original nine pound shares were valued at just two pounds, seventeen shillings and six pence. The Royal Hotel, Birmingham was regularly declared bankrupt.

Seaside hotels tended to do better, and in Bridlington the Alexandra Hotel had an advantage in that it had no rival. It therefore escaped foundering in its earlier years, while the precarious financial situation of hotels like the Cliftonville in Margate, the Burlington in Eastbourne, the Metropole in Dover, and many others, were all bought up by the Gordon's Group. This group at the end of the nineteenth century employed fifteen hundred staff and had the advantage of corporate management, purchasing and advertising, but inevitably sacrificed the personal touch in service and detailed attention to service. The Alex, mercifully, escaped being swallowed up in this corporate giant which had a reputation for raking off the profit and not reinvesting it in the properties. But seaside hotels need a number of things to thrive: tourists, no threat of war or revolution, an absence of air raids or bombardment, a good economy, full employment, confidence in the future and lots of good weather.

Following the ravages of First World War, there were huge rises in the costs of buying and transporting food and goods from overseas, and wages began to increase as workers slowly became unionised. Records from other hotels show tensions were rising behind the scenes. Directors accused managers of taking concessions from suppliers, stealing food and drink, overcharging customers, and turning a blind eye to indelicate or unsavoury visitors at night. Directors were themselves accused of forcing managers to buy from friends of the Board, taking too much profit, investing unwisely, and interfering too much in the management of the hotel. While we have no documented reason to think such difficulties were present at The Alex, any awareness of simple human dynamics and human nature means there must have been difficult meetings and relationships from time to time. Life is never calm and straightforward for anyone, especially those working in a business like hospitality.

The First World War had witnessed a quarter of the male population leave the country and far fewer return. There had been a steep rise in costs and a large drop in the availability of goods. But most seaside hotels did somehow recover, and Blackpool, Bournemouth, Scarborough and Southend all reported a welcome rise in visits from families in the 1920s. Significantly, it was in 1920 that Percy Newbound's extraordinarily ambitious plans were submitted to expand the size of the Alexandra Hotel to three times its original size. Presumably, Bridlington was also showing promising signs of recovery in the tourist trade.

But the Second World War proved much more difficult. June 1940 witnessed Operation Dynamo, the evacuation of Dunkirk. The Battle of Britain was waged that same summer. There was a very serious risk of Nazi invasion of Britain. The Home Guard was mobilised first along the south coast and then further north. Then as Holland and Scandinavia fell under German occupation, the east coast was seen as particularly vulnerable, not least Yorkshire.

Bridlington Bay was identified as especially open to attack. Its flat sandy beach was ideal for landing craft to bring tanks and gliders and troops onto the shore. The harbour might easily be brought under German control. Therefore the beaches were mined, covered with barbed wire and pillboxes, and concrete anti-landing cubes were placed at strategic points all along the coast. The remains of a number of these grim reminders can still be seen today all the way along from Thornwick Bay at Flamborough south to Hornsea and beyond, both in fields and on beaches.

Many of the hotels and guest houses in Bridlington were requisitioned by the military for the duration of the war. Children from Hull were billeted in Bridlington, arriving on the train and carrying gas masks and identity cards in their cases. The streets were often filled with troops guarding the routes from the beach, with tank traps and all sorts of military vehicles.

For the duration of the war the huge Alexandra Hotel became an overspill Logistics Training School when the top RAF College, Cranwell, became overcrowded. Central throughout all the wartime activities was the efficient movement of personnel and equipment. So those training here were being educated in the project management of making sure everything and everyone was in the right place at the right time for every day of the war: aircraft, fuel, spare parts, weapons, ammunition, communication equipment, uniforms, food, mobile kitchens and hospitals – the list is endless. All this was in addition to the routine gunnery practice and so on.

Yorkshire had no fewer than fifty-five RAF airfields, several of which were within very easy reach of the town: Bempton (radar), Carnaby (emergency landing strip for crippled aircraft), Driffield (training bomber crews), Full Sutton, Holme on Spalding Moor, and Lissett (all under Bomber Command), Elvington (also a base for the Free French Forces), Leconfield (fighter unit including Spitfires), and Catfoss (Spitfires, training, and a base for coastal command).

For obvious reasons of national security, there is scant evidence of what really went on within the walls of The Alex, and we can also only imagine the feelings of the owners and staff as the military took over. Were they emotions of willing acceptance at best, dutiful resignation, or resentment at worst? At a functional level, fine furniture would have been labelled and moved and no doubt the dance floor suffered from heavy boots. Smart bedrooms would have been used as stark offices where secret plans of air defence and attack were discussed. Hotel staff would have been laid off or reassigned. Cellars no doubt became bunkers, safe havens from enemy action as bombs were dropped on the town and harbour deliberately, or simply jettisoned as German aeroplanes made their way back to the continent. There are second-hand tales of target practice and pistol training on the front lawn of the hotel, part of which was transformed into an assault course, but we are left to imagine most of what those six years held.

With all this going on, it is especially difficult to imagine in particular the real feelings of the owners, the Hatje family. William Hatje who bought the hotel in the 1930s was originally from Hamburg in Germany (as we noted earlier), but he died just before the outbreak of war in 1938. His sons Walter and Norman took over the running of The Alex, and with such an obviously European name they would have been under constant, if discreet, surveillance during a time of understandable nationalistic paranoia. In London alone, thousands of people in the catering and food industries with German and Italian-sounding names were rounded up for interrogation and many sent to internment camps. Indeed, William Hatje himself had been interned during the First World War, leaving his wife Isabella to bring up their five children and run their current hotel, The Grand in Wick, Caithness, Scotland, single handed.

The family would inevitably have had relatives still in Germany, and to this day Hatje remains a prominent surname in and around

Hamburg with many such people holding distinguished positions in their professions. Whatever William's reasons for emigrating to Scotland years earlier, his family must have had many conflicts of emotion churning in their hearts as they witnessed England at war with their family's homeland, Germany.

What must have been so very hard for members of the Hatje family would have been the devastating RAF bombing of the city of Hamburg itself. Hamburg was a major industrial city and therefore a prime target during the war. Allied attacks on the shipyards, U-boat pens and oil refineries were carried out constantly. In July 1943, "Operation Gomorrah" (named after the devastation of the city of Gomorrah by brimstone and fire in the Bible [Genesis 19]) was the heaviest air assault ever launched to date. So heavy was the firestorm raised from the incessant bombing that a tornado of fire four hundred and sixty metres high was recorded. Throughout the war over twenty-two thousand tons of bombs were dropped on the city destroying nearly six hundred arms factories. An estimated forty-two thousand civilians were killed, thirty-seven thousand wounded, and over a million fled the city. Hitler declared that if this level of destruction continued then defeat was certain.

Walter and Norman Hatje must have reflected on the fact that the British RAF were working on these sorts of bombing raids from local airfields while based in their very own requisitioned hotel, The Alex. This must have been extraordinarily difficult for them, and we can hardly begin to guess at how they coped with this conflict of emotions and loyalties, inevitably wondering about the fate of some of their own relatives.

War, however, inevitably brings conflicts of all sorts other than the obvious battle between opposing sides. Even locally, we are bound to wonder, what was the nature of practical human activity within The Alex itself? How did all the service men and women really get on, drawn as they were from different backgrounds and from all over the country? How did different personalities get on when suddenly forced together? What damaged emotions came to the fore when people had to focus on a common task that brought scarred memories out into the open? What romances blossomed into marriage as time went on? What liaisons took place despite marriages back at home? What relationships across the ranks made giving and receiving orders difficult? All we can do is imagine, but could all this form the basis of a very colourful television drama series just waiting to be made?

During the war all hotels suffered severe neglect and some inevitable vandalism of their architecture. Expensive cutlery had been misused and personalised crockery chipped. Considerable repairs and renovations were needed, and in any case the troops did not leave immediately in 1945. Bridlington's North Beach was closed until 1949 and The Alex could not re-open for business until the hotel was restored and the beach cleared and declared safe in April 1949. One photograph shows a concrete pillbox situated at the foot of the steps from neighbouring Alexandra Walk onto the Promenade – hardly an enticing sight for holidaymakers who not only wanted to forget the war, but could now begin to look to the Mediterranean for an escape into a different sort of holiday experience.

Increasingly, the owners of grand hotels throughout the country became the live-in managers, and staffs were reduced in numbers.

Huge expenses were incurred as some tried to modernise, but drilling through solid Victorian walls to install modern central heating was likened to trying to "modify the Rock of Gibraltar" (Lord Stamp, speaking about the Midland Grand Hotel at St Pancras).

Some seaside towns tried to reinvent themselves as conference centres, with their old large hotels able to provide the necessary accommodation. Brighton, Bournemouth and Blackpool all had some success with this, and just before the war Bridlington was the venue for the Trades Union Congress Conference in 1939, but the war seemed to place a halt on any such subsequent development. In passing, it might be of interest to note that at the 1939 TUC Conference the important "Bridlington Agreement" was passed. This legislation remains very important for the unity of the Trade Union movement, as it forbids the poaching of members from one union by another, and is often quoted to this day.

Successive governments have often seemed unable to recognise seaside tourism as an important but invisible part of the national economy, and consequently many resorts with their grand hotels have struggled to flourish in a harsh and unsupported economic climate. The hospitality business has always been both exciting and exhilarating, but also brutal and unforgiving at the same time. The fact that the various owners, managers and staff managed to keep The Alex open for over a century surely demands loud applause. It was always "jolly hard work", but very obviously much appreciated by the thousands of guests whose lives were enhanced by the experience of such a grand hotel.

24. THE TIFFANY YEARS

The 1960s was a hugely significant decade for everyone. After the austerity of the Second World War and then post-war rationing, a new generation was determined to enjoy a much greater sense of freedom. Attitudes to absolutely every aspect of culture changed. Fashion, food, music, leisure, relationships, education, work patterns would all never be the same again. The establishment was rocked as the old order was challenged and satirised as never before. It was an exciting, liberating, tumultuous and breathless era that defined a generation.

Right in the middle of these "swinging sixties", 1965 was a momentous year. One hundred and twenty-five thousand American soldiers landed for the first time in Vietnam. Astronaut Ed White became the first human being to walk in space. The death penalty was abolished in England, and The Race Relations Act became law. In the cinemas blockbusters like "The Sound of Music", "Dr Zhivago" and "Help!" all hit the screens. Three hundred and twenty-one thousand people filed past the coffin of Sir Winston Churchill before his state funeral. Natural gas was struck in the North Sea. The Post Office Tower in London opened, and The Beatles made their final live tour, ending in Cardiff. Every single day the newspapers' front pages bore headlines which were either life-changing or totally captivating with articles about a new discovery, invention, scandal or movement.

In the middle of all this excitement and turmoil, the leisure and holiday industry was also changing out of all recognition. The Alexandra Hotel had become increasingly difficult to manage as a profitable business as people looked at different possibilities. Package holidays overseas, and holiday camps and caravans at home, all beckoned. So in February 1965 the Hatje family sold The Alex to Stanley and Alice Tiffany.

The hotel was, again, acquired as a complete family business. Stanley and Alice bought the hotel, and their three daughters and husbands (Pauline and Jim, Janice and Les, Ann and Gerry) were all directors who were totally involved in the day to day management of every aspect of its life.

Stanley and Alice were already running The Hammerton Hotel in Kirk Hammerton, about ten miles west of York, and they continued to do so, usually visiting The Alex once a week to check that everything was going smoothly. Pauline, who later became a gourmet chef, ran the kitchens. She had learnt the trade at The Hotel and Catering College in Huddersfield, which prior to her being accepted had been a male-only college. Immediately before coming to The Alex she had taught at The Flagler College, St Augustine, Florida. Hygiene was uppermost in her priorities. Janice ran the housekeeping, and Jim the bars. Ann was in charge of the dining room and Les oversaw reception, front of house and the accounts.

They bought the hotel in February for £38,000 and opened it just weeks later on Good Friday, April 16th 1965. A vast amount of money was spent renovating it from top to bottom at a manic speed. Tophams of Bridlington worked all round the clock on the internal decorations. Brian Chinnery, who had only recently set up in business, fashioned all the woodwork and joinery. Sinclairs had the contract for the external painting, which alone cost over four thousand pounds. Ron Ford worked on the plumbing, and the electrical work was undertaken by Fox's of Rothwell, who were friends of the family. The man working on the roofing is remembered as sitting on the second floor balcony scratching his head with his trowel, causing the new owners considerable anxiety!

Hunters and Smallpage of York were involved in the design and supply of internal refurbishments. All new mattresses and bedding were bought to fit the existing bedsteads. The bathrooms and Victorian toilets were brought back to sparkling condition, and the sumptuous red velvet curtains were nothing short of luxurious. All the catering equipment, cutlery and crockery were supplied by Molletts of Bradford.

It was a huge and very expensive task, systematically tackled floor by floor. When The Alex was re-opened the first floor and some of the second floor rooms were initially ready for occupation, with the ground floor dining room, ballroom, reception and the two bars all renovated to a very high specification. The project-management skills needed were very considerable.

But the Tiffanys were a talented and hard-working family. Stanley, an electrical engineer by background, was a strict perfectionist but very kind. He played the piano well and was also able to play any musical instrument placed in front of him. From 1945-1950 he was the Labour Cooperative Member of Parliament for Peterborough and later served on Wakefield Council, eventually becoming Leader of the Council. He was awarded the CBE in 1967, four years before he died in 1971.

Alice was also musically very talented, and always to be found singing. With her, too, everything had to be just right. The menus had to be good and varied, and except for breakfast all meals were silver service.

Just one example of the demands and surprises involved in running a large hotel involved Les, one of their sons-in-law, who hated heights. On one particularly windy day, the flag which displayed the words "The Alexandra Hotel" as it flew above the roof, became entangled in the television aerial. Summoning all his courage, he climbed out of a skylight onto the roof to tear it free leaving the words "The Alex" flying proudly, a challenge neither he nor his family ever forgot!

Inevitably, in order to maintain the hotel as a viable business, hard work was always the order of the day, and it could be demanding for all the staff at every level. Often, two large wedding receptions might be held at the same time, one in the dining room and one in the ballroom, keeping a large staff on their feet for all the hours of the day as well as long into the night.

In order to keep the hotel fully booked both in and out of season, all sorts of special packages were offered. Christmas Breaks, for example, were tightly packed programmes: Champagne buffets, masked balls, trips to see fox-hunts out in the country, film shows, Father Christmas for the children, and so on were all advertised to attract customers. This meant there was no time off for the staff, with that constant pressure to fill each day with a wide variety of events for all ages.

The reception desk was very strictly controlled by Miss Sharpe, alternating with the less austere Paddy Senior. Vaughan Boddy was the uniformed assistant hall porter and was a model employee. He was always polite, trustworthy and willing, and went on to work in a large London hotel. His father also worked at The Alex as the gardener. Mr Carter was the chef, and Toni was the perfectionist head-waiter. Johnny Smith was the ever-popular cocktail waiter, assisted by older barman, Harold Smallwood. During the busy summer season well over fifty people were employed, with extra staff being taken on for special functions. The Alexandra Hotel was a major employer in Bridlington, and very important for the local economy.

Some of the special functions were more memorable than others, and not always for the best of reasons. For example, the members of "The Ladies' Licensed Victuallers Association" had a reputation for being by far the heaviest drinkers, with their never-ending requests throughout the evening for yet another "triple gin and tonic" at the bar. Their annual celebration at the hotel became the subject of a lot of gossip in the town!

Some of the Tiffanys' overnight guests were equally memorable, but all for different reasons. Those playing as headline acts at The Spa often stayed at The Alex. There were a number of occasions when all-male pop groups who invited large numbers of female groupies back for the night had to be told in no uncertain terms to leave. But on the other hand, top pop group The Rolling Stones, feared by parents for breaking all the conventional rules, were always very polite and pleasantly behaved. In the morning they would go for an early run on the beach, and back at the hotel would be happy relaxing with a cup of tea.

A London based group, "The Stones" formed in 1962 and consisted of Mick Jagger, Keith Richards, Brian Jones, Bill Wyman and Ian Stewart. Symbolic of the youth counterculture of the sixties their music was a synthesis of blues and rock, with huge world-wide hits such as "I can't get no satisfaction", "Nineteenth nervous breakdown", "Get off of my cloud", "Lady Jane", "Ruby Tuesday", "Little red rooster", "Jumping Jack Flash", "Let's spend the night together" … the list is endless. To this day they still tour globally playing in huge stadiums with the earliest original members Mick Jagger and Keith Richards joined by Ronnie Wood and Charlie Watts. They have now sold over two hundred and fifty million albums and collected scores of top awards. It shows the amazing vibrancy of Bridlington at that time to be able to attract such groups, and the very high calibre of The Alexandra Hotel to be the place they chose to stay.

Birmingham based group The Moody Blues were also welcomed as guests by the Tiffanys. They were at the forefront of what became known as "Brumbeat", with their progressive style of rock music. Formed in 1964 they quickly made their mark in the charts with numbers such as "Nights in white satin", "Tuesday afternoon" and "Go now" and have totalled over seventy million album sales to their credit. They are still performing today, featuring on the '60s nostalgia circuit so popular all around the country, and even now these shows fill every seat with those who remember them from their heyday. In fact, today when The Spa advertises a "sixties" show, it usually also means the audience will be at least in their sixties!

Another top sixties group to stay at The Alex in their heyday was The Hollies, who also still perform around the country today. Formed in 1962 in Manchester, their distinctive three-part vocal harmony gave them two hundred and thirty-one weeks in the charts during the sixties, and they were the ninth highest charting artists of the decade. Again, that says a lot about the status of both the town and the hotel in those days to be able to host them. Their enduring successes include "Bus stop", "Just one look", "Look through any window", "I can't let go", "On a carousel", "Jennifer Eccles", "Carrie Anne", "He ain't heavy he's my brother" and "The air that I breathe." Together with the Rolling Stones they are one of the few groups of that era never to have disbanded.

The Swinging Blue Jeans, originally a skiffle group from Liverpool, began to make their mark in 1962 and majored in rock and roll. Their appearances on stage with hits like "Hippy hippy shake", "Good golly Miss Molly", "You're no good" and "Don't make me over" still draw a full audience at The Spa nearly sixty years later, though these days the group no longer contains any of the original members who stayed at The Alex all those years ago.

Top comedians also stayed at The Alex. At the very pinnacle of the nation's entertainment were Morecambe and Wise. Eric Morecambe (1926 – 84) and Ernie Wise (1925 - 99) were the iconic comic double act who conquered variety and music halls, then radio, then television and even the cinema, continually rising in popularity from their beginnings in 1941 right through to 1984. Put simply, they were the best-loved double act of all time. Morecambe was the bumbling buffoon and Wise the straight man who between them spawned national catchphrases such as "Short fat hairy legs", "The play what I wrote", "Tea Ern?", "That's easy for you to say" and so many more.

The "Morecambe and Wise Christmas Specials" on television drew not only the most memorable guests such as Glenda Jackson, Cliff Richard, Elton John and Angela Rippon who were overjoyed to join them and be mocked in their sketches, but the shows drew record television audiences of over twenty million between 1969 and 1980. Hilarious dialogue such as that between Eric Morecambe and top international conductor Andre Previn ("Look sunshine, I'm playing all the right notes but not necessarily in the right order!"), their wonderfully funny conversations as they sat up in bed together with no hint of impropriety, their fabulous kitchen sketch to the tune of "The Stripper" as they prepared breakfast, and their signature song "Bring me sunshine" have all stood the test of time in a way that bears an undeniable testimony to their brilliance.

When Eric Morecambe stayed in The Alex while appearing at The Spa, the Tiffanys always remember him as an extremely pleasant man who appreciated simply being treated as a normal everyday person. He put on no airs and graces and certainly wanted no deference. Ernie Wise would join him for breakfast.

On one occasion Eric Morecambe invited Janice Tiffany to share a bottle of wine with him as he did not like drinking alone, and sat her two-year-old daughter, Amanda, on his knee as they chatted together

– a relaxed and special memory treasured by their family to this day, and a lovely picture of the efficient but warm and relaxed atmosphere they created for guests as they ran The Alex.

Having worked so hard to keep The Alex a place of fun and enjoyment for hundreds of people, things came to a fairly abrupt end, however. An accident to a family member meant that it was no longer possible to carry on, and the hotel was sold after only two years to Mr Crocker in March 1967. During that short time it had been brought up to a very good condition, and was handed on as a very healthy economic proposition.

While in those two short years a lot had happened within the walls of The Alex, even more was happening in the wider world. In 1967 the Six Days' War exploded in the Middle East reshaping international boundaries. Nearly half a million soldiers were now serving in Vietnam as that war escalated in a way no one had imagined. "The Graduate" and "Bonnie and Clyde" were released in cinemas. Twiggy burst on the scene as an international supermodel with her unique new brand of short haircut, large eyes and waif-like appearance, and The Beatles continued to reign supreme releasing "Sgt Pepper's Lonely Hearts Club Band". This was the year of the "Summer of Love", when the hippy revolution and "flower power" began to take hold in America and spread into Britain.

North Sea Gas was now being pumped ashore for the first time, bringing a new prosperity with it, but the Torrey Canyon oil spill was a dreadful ecological disaster when the tanker ran aground at sea near Land's End in Cornwall. British Steel was nationalised and colour television was broadcast for the first time by the BBC. Sandie

Shaw won the Eurovision Song Contest with "Puppet on a String". For young children a new style of programmes like "Trumpton" appeared on BBC Television, while "The Forsyte Saga" captured the adult population on Sunday evenings. At every level and for every age-group these were staggeringly exciting times.

No wonder the two short years the Tiffany family owned The Alexandra Hotel reads like a breathless sprint – and what an era in which to run a large and busy hotel!

25. TWO DIFFERENT CAREERS SET IN MOTION?

In the kitchens of a hotel, a commis-chef is a junior member of staff on the first rung of the ladder in training to be a great chef. In most kitchens the work involves preparing food, doing basic cooking under the watchful eye of the head chef, gaining experience in the various types of cooking, and cleaning and looking after kitchen equipment. It can mean long hours, strict discipline, a willingness to learn on the job, and an ability to work in a team.

Here we have two different stories from two young men who each worked for a short time as a commis-chef in The Alex, one from the 1950s and one from the 1970s. They each illustrate two things: first, that the conditions changed out of all recognition over the years; and second, that working at The Alex could play a crucial part in determining a person's path and career through the rest of their lives.

In June 1958, an eighteen-year-old Rod Lewis moved from Doncaster to live in and work as a commis-chef at The Alex. His half-brother, Jim, was the Head Chef, and Rod enjoyed living in his own room on the ground floor in the staff accommodation. He remembers fondly enjoying sunbathing on the roof, appreciating the rose beds in front of the hotel and working with his brother. But while he was at The Alex, something very dramatic happened which was to change his life.

Rod writes: "Just before my sixteenth birthday I had become a born-again Christian. I had been invited by an elderly lady to come and hear a former communist give his testimony in the local church. That night I went forward to give my life to Jesus Christ. I experienced the tangible love of God.

When I came to Bridlington I needed some Christian fellowship and met a couple called Mr & Mrs Weston who encouraged me to seek the baptism in the Holy Spirit. This I did. One August evening after work I crossed the road to the beach and attended a mission led by Methodist Cliff Trekkers (groups of staff and students from Cliff Methodist Bible College in the Peak District). The leader, Jim Beales, preached on the story of Pentecost (in the Bible, Acts of the Apostles 2: 1 – 4) where it says the early Christians were 'all filled with the Holy Spirit and began to speak in other languages as the Spirit gave them utterance.' I went forward to receive this powerful gift.

"As I sat on that seawall and Jim Beales laid hands on me I experienced the tangible fire of the awesome Holy Spirit, and from that moment my life has gone from glory to glory. I expect if I took you to that spot on the seawall today you would still see the scorch mark!"

Rod says the very next day he walked around Bridlington telling anyone who would listen about what had happened to him, and inviting them to "come to know the Lord Jesus as your personal saviour, Lord, healer and baptiser in the Holy Spirit." Just one year later, aged nineteen, Rod became a local preacher and has been a Christian minister, evangelist and pastor ever since. At the time of writing he pastors a Pentecostal Church in Burntwood, Staffordshire

(The New Life Church, Cannock Road, Burntwood) – all as a result of working from June to September 1958 as a commis-chef at The Alex.

From reading Rod's story it is evident that working at the hotel has a very warm place in his heart, and for a whole host of reasons he has reason to be grateful for his time there.

Working at The Alex in the 1950s, however, was very different to working there some years later. The hotel ownership had moved from Mr & Mrs Hatje and through Mr Tiffany to Mr and Mrs Crocker. The hotel trade was passing through hard times, and the days of the old grand hotels were numbered. Standards of service, not least in the kitchens, were very different.

Steve Pepper worked also as a commis-chef at The Alex, but fourteen years later than Rod Lewis, in 1972. A lot had changed. He writes: "The Alexandra Hotel was already in decline, and the car park at the front had the remainder of a once-gracious garden. The Crockers were the owners, but the building was in a generally poor state by then. They had invested in a new kitchen but the top floor and staffing areas had plenty of missing windows, and pigeons could often be found roosting in the spare rooms. You could smell them!

"I only stopped there for about eight months and was shocked at what I saw, having come from a very sheltered upbringing. The staff included a number of people, both gay and straight, who had various relationships with each other, some openly boasting and embarrassing each other publicly about their activities.

"One barman developed a relationship with one of the waitresses.

They went on one of the pleasure steamers on their day off and he proposed to her. She accepted and they bought a cheap engagement ring from Woolworths. The next thing we knew was that they had left, taking money from the cash till and leaving on IOU in it. You couldn't make it up!

"Looking at the front of the building, the single storey building to the left was a dance hall with a sprung floor. The right-hand side was the main dining area. Johnny's cocktail bar was just on the right at the front of the hotel reception area and probably covered three front windows.

"One older night porter once answered the telephone by singing 'There ain't nobody here but us chickens', which I suspect was an old music hall or variety song. He also produced a business card which said something along the lines of, 'I'm not as good as I once was, but I am as good once as I ever was.' He used to give it to the women he would meet on his nights off.

"One of the younger waitresses once asked the chef if she could taste the paté he was making. He agreed, so she got a spoon to try it. She didn't like it, so she spat it back into the bowl. If my memory serves me right, it was used rather than thrown out!

"The head chef would often check the safety of the food organoleptically, i.e. if it didn't smell too bad it was used, and if it had started to turn it would be used in a spicy dish such as a curry. Even then this head chef would drink twenty-odd pints a day and he probably ended up a long-term alcoholic. The last time I saw him in the 1980s he was working on the oil rigs looking extremely worse for wear, asking in a pub for a bottle of whisky.

"The food hygiene left a lot to be desired. The old hotplate area (from the 1930s) was a bit of a no-man's land regarding food safety, with waiters coming in the kitchen, stubbing out their fag-ends and kicking them under the hotplates. There was quite a pile of fag-ends I remember.

"The hotel was busy on a weekend with Saturday night dances being very popular, but the number of residents was very low. Some of them were elderly and were using the hotel as a place of residence rather than going into a nursing home. Amongst others, I remember Anthony Wedgewood-Benn's father there.

"I never worked in the hotel trade again, choosing to work in the welfare sector of catering (care homes, NHS etc). I eventually became the manager (which included responsibility for catering) of a single homeless hostel in Wakefield, which often gave me a sense of déjà-vu from my days at the Alexandra Hotel.

"Most of the employees at the hotel lived in and were very transient, stopping only for a month or two before moving on. Most of the customers or visitors would have been horrified, had they been aware how the staff behaved, and the poor standards behind the scenes."

Steve Pepper certainly has given a very vivid and rich description of life behind the scenes in 1972! That in itself is fascinating and brings the story of the hotel to life. What is also fascinating, given his words about the standards in the kitchen, is that he has gone on to gain some impressive and not-unrelated qualifications: he is a Fellow of the Royal Society for Public Health, the highest membership grade of the society, and a Member of the Institute for Hospitality, having gained the appropriate qualifications, training and experience at a senior management level in the hospitality industry.

No one working at The Alex in 1972 under those dreadful conditions would have imagined this junior commis-chef would, forty-five years later, be training others in Health and Safety and Higher Level Food safety.

Rod Lewis and Steve Pepper both worked as commis-chefs at The Alex, but at different times and under different regimes. Both went on to paths of life and careers where undoubtedly the experience of being there was very profound. How many more stories are there where people's lives were shaped, at least in part, by this place? We may never know, but these two contrasting descriptions give us at least a clue of the range of stories, the effect of which will still be being felt by many, many people.

26. THE FINAL CURTAIN

Biologists, historians and archaeologists each tell us that those species of animals which fail to respond to their changing circumstances, all eventually become extinct. Animals need to adapt and change to suit a new environment or meet a new challenge. They develop legs, a long neck, dextrous fingers, better eyesight or hearing, or larger brains. That way they emerge as the victor over a changing climate or food availability, or even over other competitive animals. It is about survival of the fittest, the most agile.

The story of the grand seaside hotel is no different. They were first built as a result of the coming of the railways, the demand for a good home in pleasant surroundings, and an escape from the noisy masses. They were built to demonstrate British solidarity and stoutness – large, firm, unmoveable.

But this meant they were not agile. Their thick permanent walls did not lend themselves to adaptation when later waves of different holidaymakers demanded en-suites, easily controlled heating, and cheap prices. These big old hotels could not evolve to meet the holiday revolution happening all around them.

Sadly, as the progress of the twentieth century marched relentlessly forward, one after the other of these grand institutions began to fall by the wayside, increasingly looking like dinosaurs from a bygone age. The Alex adapted as far as it could, and for a time seemed to do well, but as the years went by the struggle became more demanding.

During the First World War it became obvious that coastal resorts were vulnerable to enemy attacks. On December 16th 1914, nearby Scarborough was bombarded by five hundred shells before similar attention was paid to Whitby and Hartlepool, provoking outrage at this deliberate attack on civilians. The Grand Hotel in Scarborough suffered direct hits from shells resulting in damage that cost ten thousand pounds to repair. The seaside suddenly seemed less attractive. Many men were away and many never returned. Money was less available. An article in The Yorkshire Weekly Post described Bridlington as a "town deserted...only three couples on the dance floor." Hotels and boarding houses were used for military purposes. Beaches became training grounds. Minesweepers could be seen among the fishing boats. Foreign nationals were frowned upon as guests.

After the war, business did recover and visitors returned, but surrounding smaller hotels began more easily and cheaply to upgrade their standards with modern connections to gas, electricity and water supplies, and so challenged the assumed superiority of the larger establishments.

As fashions changed, so women's swimming costumes developed from the nineteenth century swimwear, through shorter costumes with little modesty skirts, eventually to the bikini. The rubber swimming caps came and went. Men wore trunks, later ranging from Bermuda shorts to tiny Speedos, and everyone simply got changed under a towel. Even being able to advertise that guests could hire a bathing machine from the hotel now seemed absurd.

It was no longer enough to boast "a smoking room and a drawing room." Publicity began to have to refer to the proximity of a garage and petrol for cars. The rows of coaches parked behind the hotel in one of the photographs tell their own story.

Because the hotel was requisitioned by the R.A.F. during the Second World War, inevitably a degree of customer loyalty and reputation was lost. The Alex had suffered no direct damage, although St Anne's Orphanage and Convalescent Home in the next street caught a direct hit from a parachute land mine on the 18th January 1941.

This parachute mine that landed on St Anne's Convalescent Home completely destroyed it outright. A second parachute mine landed just a few yards further away on the corner of Eighth Avenue and Lamplugh Road. Here, thirteen houses were destroyed and others damaged beyond repair. Twenty people were trapped, of whom thirteen were rescued and seven killed. These two enormous explosions were from just two land mines, each weighing a thousand kilograms, measuring eight feet long and descending at forty miles an hour. After being dropped from the aeroplane, a parachute would open to slow the descent of the mines so that the aeroplane could fly as far away as possible to escape the enormous blast. When they hit the ground, a timer would be activated to detonate the explosion twenty-five seconds later. They were lethal and terrifying.

It is highly probable that the enormous blast from these explosions explains the wartime photograph of the hotel showing all the rear windows shattered, much of the roof damaged, and many of the outbuildings at the back wrecked.

When the hotel eventually did reopen in April 1949 things were different. It was hard to begin all over again. The aftermath of war meant rationing, austerity, and little spare cash for luxuries like nostalgic holidays in expensive hotels for most people.

Bridlington as a seaside resort began to change as a result. Day-trippers began to replace those who previously might have stayed for a week. Different attractions were needed for those who only came for a few hours rather than a number of days. Caravan sites sprung up. Nearby Butlins Holiday Camp at Filey flourished. Self-catering became an economic option.

The rise in car ownership meant people could travel to where they wished, rather than just where the railway took them. In 1965 the direct railway line to York was closed, which both reflected the decline in visitors, but also resulted in encouraging further that very decline. In 1966 Bridlington railway station had 440,000 passengers, but the following year in 1967 there were only 205,000. Only the development of the Bessingby and Carnaby industrial estates stopped the line from being closed completely.

Three cinemas closed: The Lounge in 1961, The Roxy in 1962, and The Regal (ABC) in 1971. Two large hotels, The Victoria and The Promenade, were demolished. Boarding houses became cheaply rented multi-occupancy dwellings, The Pavilion became Jerome's, and the Grand Pavilion Theatre made way for the "Three Bs" Leisure World (demolished in 2013).

The huge Alexandra Hotel was bound to struggle. Rooms were not as regularly refurbished as they had been previously. The furniture and décor became tired. Rooms were offered more cheaply to keep visitors coming, but consequently the revenue fell. People complained the rooms were always cold. Single events like wedding receptions flourished, Saturday night dances were well attended, hospital balls were fun, organisations held their annual celebrations, meetings were accommodated, and children's parties were memorable, but the huge number of bedrooms were no longer anything like full. Behind the scenes things were not going at all well. Terrie Britt remembers working there for a holiday job over Whitsun 1968, when the infestation of rats was so bad that many of the staff simply walked out, refusing to return to work for the summer season

Valiant attempts were made to keep The Alex alive in a new age. The last owner, Billy Compton, tried to resurrect it as a disco and night club. Pop Groups played at various events, among them the chart topping Barron Knights who came in the 1970s. This is a fun-loving group founded in 1959, and still playing the cabaret circuit to this day. In their early years they were a supporting act to both the Beatles and the Rolling Stones, and they stormed the charts at number 3 in 1964 with "Here come the groups", a parody of leading groups of the time including The Searchers, Freddy and the Dreamers, the Dave Clark Five and the Bachelors. They had two more hits with "Pop go the workers" (1965) and "Merrie gentle pops" (1966), but their biggest hit came in 1978 with "A taste of Agro." With a total of fourteen chart hits to their name, to book them to play at a struggling hotel like The Alex in the 1970s was a brave and ambitious thing to have done.

Then a second great challenge came. Workers' pay began to improve, but cheap overseas package holidays were now being offered. People could now go to countries like Spain with guaranteed sunshine, and stay in a modern hotel with private bathrooms, a hot buffet with lots of choice of food, a swimming pool with sunbeds, and organised "kids clubs". The figures speak for themselves: in 1960 there were four million foreign holiday flights, in 1970 it was seven million, and by 2000 it was forty-five million. If these holidays were offered in hotels resembling concrete blocks, then so be it. People no longer looked for ornate architecture. Now it was about function rather than form. Old hotels like The Alex were hard to modernise because their construction was so solid – the very thing that had made them so appealing at first.

In the country as a whole this challenge was met by new chain hotels such as Trusthouse Forte and Butlins, who bought old, large hotels and managed them all centrally. Later came Holiday Inn, Britannia, and then Travelodge who could all purchase everything in bulk, and negotiate cheap contracts with suppliers of everything from food, laundry and advertising though to maintenance, recruitment and furnishings. It was impossible to compete.

In turn, those hotels of all sizes and types which did remain independent, and those swallowed up by the big chains, both began to turn to new concepts like weekend and short breaks, but these could not bring in revenue that matched the old days.

Holidaymakers are not philanthropic supporters of past glories. They want value for money. This is not greed, it is just common sense. It was the same drive that had nudged the original shareholders to invest in building The Alex in the first place. The investors a hundred years earlier were driven by a desire for a good return for their money which succeeded by offering people a good time in the process.

The problem was that the wealthy who came in the early years, came precisely to escape the working masses. The wealthy now left for more exotic holidays. The middle classes began to leave for Spain. Those with less spare money came to Bridlington but now just for the day or they stayed in caravans or cheaper guest houses. It was a pincer movement that began to strangle the huge hotel.

The final blow came with the fires of the 1970s, the first of which in 1973 claimed the life of a member of staff who, it was said, fell asleep in bed and his cigarette started the fire. The fire wrecked the south wing and destroyed part of the roof. Repairs cost forty-three thousand pounds, and even then much of the hotel had to remain out of bounds and so brought in no income.

The second fire in 1975 was surrounded by even more controversy. The hotel was now owned by Mrs Margaret Williamene (Billy) Compton of The Chalet, Seaton Sands, Longniddry, East Lothian, who described herself as an office manager. On the night before the formal closure of the hotel in 1975, there was a great farewell dinner with people sat around tables, but unlike that wonderful dinner on its opening night in 1866, the guests this time had to bring their own drinks. That in itself is an indication of the sad state of affairs.

The Alex and its land were then put up for auction. The auctioneer confirmed that a tender was subsequently accepted but could not disclose the purchaser or the price paid. All we know is that the hotel had previously been sold for one hundred and ten thousand pounds in 1973, but was now valued at only sixty thousand pounds when the hotel was finally sold. The owner, Mrs "Billy" Compton, filed her petition for bankruptcy in that same year, 1975.

According to the Bridlington Free Press, in September that year, fire engines were again called to the hotel. A fire had mysteriously broken out and the blaze destroyed two hundred square feet of the roof. The fire itself took only twenty minutes to extinguish but the damage caused by the flames and then the water from the hoses was all very extensive. It was claimed young people had been sleeping in the empty hotel, but the top floor had been closed for some years because of holes in the roof and the derelict state of the rooms there. At the time, there was much talk in the town about the mysterious tangle of the hotel's closure, a file for bankruptcy, a very low valuation of the hotel, the undisclosed auction figure, the fire, and then demolition the following year – 1976. Perhaps there were no connections at all, but conspiracy theories have a habit of not disappearing.

While all of this was going on, a lot of discussion was happening behind closed doors. The Borough Council had often expressed an interest in buying the hotel and all the land. The Yorkshire Dales Housing Association proposed retaining the hotel frontage and developing a very ambitious scheme which would keep fifty-two bedrooms, and offer bars, conference rooms, a variety of housing and some shops. However, nothing came of these proposals probably in part because a loan from the Council would have been needed to enable this two million pounds venture. In the end, it was finally sold by sealed tender for an undisclosed amount."

So, the once-glorious Alexandra Hotel had come to a very undignified end. Perhaps it was all inevitable.

Today, however, two questions remain. First, would permission now be given for the Alexandra Hotel to be demolished? Heritage bodies are powerful lobbies and historic buildings are notoriously difficult when it comes to disposal. Might the impressive frontage have been retained as a Listed Building, with perhaps new seaside apartments created behind? This sort of solution is always extremely expensive and rarely very satisfactory, but it does sometimes happen.

Second, if the hotel had managed to survive, what might it be offering? Today, grand old hotels in seaside resorts tend to have been bought by companies such as Britannia, Warners, Butlins, and Shearings. Budget holidays, mid-week specials, pre-Christmas Tinsel and Turkey, and Twixmas Breaks (the days between Christmas and New Year) all feature in their brochures. Daily coach trips and evening entertainment comprising Bingo and Cabaret are all appreciated by the visiting older age groups.

It is easy to be dismissive of this trend, but strangely it is not too far removed from the original concept of the Alexandra Hotel, created by its shareholders all those years ago. What is offered is not so much a "resort centred" but rather a "hotel centred" holiday, where the hotel itself can organise everything the guest could possibly want. Once upon a time it was a bathing machine and a theatre ticket, and now it is a coach excursion during the day and a comedian during the evening.

Understood this way, the sort of holidays offered by The Alex are now no longer the exclusive preserve of the wealthy, but are available to a much wider spectrum of people through any travel agent, internet site or magazine advertisement. In its own way, this is surely a very healthy development. It is nothing less than the democratisation of the hotel holiday.

(v) A GENEROUS LEGACY

27. THANKS FOR THE MEMORY

The Alexandra Hotel had come to the end of its life before the age of the Internet revolutionised our lives. Today we can find information, buy goods, book holidays and search for lost friends, all at the tap on a keyboard. It is a two-edged sword.

On the negative side, we can join groups like Facebook, and "befriend" or "unfriend" people we have never met with just the click of a button. This is so unlike the earlier days of The Alex when people would come for a holiday, physically meet new people, and gradually get to know each other, sometimes embarking then on a whole life together.

On the positive side, we have wonderful groups on Facebook like "Bridlington The Good Old Days". When a short appeal for memories of The Alex was posted in 2018, within seconds people had started to respond. Over the next two weeks well over a hundred people offered their memories and anecdotes.

What is very noticeable is that, for obvious reasons, all those who responded are living and therefore their memories are more recent, often of the hotel when it was past its glory days. Yet nearly all the comments were extremely warm and affectionate. Even when things were not as they once were, The Alex obviously still played a really important part in people's lives.

When the appeal was made, the request was that those responding would make it clear whether or not they were happy to be identified with their remarks. Few did, either way, so a further appeal was made for any to say if they specifically did not want their names or comments shared. Again, there was no surge of responses. Consequently, to stay on the safe side, comments recorded here have been grouped according to subject matter. The various authors have then been thanked in simple alphabetical order in the acknowledgements at the end of the book. This hopefully spares the blushes of the innocent and protects the guilty! Those who think they recognise any of these names, or who enjoy detective work, might try to connect the comment to the name. Others can simply marvel at the nostalgic love that simply oozes from those words.

Some loved it: "absolutely beautiful building"… "why was this knocked down"… "I loved that hotel"… "such a beautiful building – a shame it was knocked down"… "a great old place".

A number worked at the hotel for a time: "I worked there as a chamber maid and waitress, 1972-73"… "my mum was a chamber maid in the '50s"… "I remember working there in 1974 – the place was falling to bits"… "my friend's dad was the chef there"… "in the early days I used to carry the cases a lot to The Alex, and then when I was eighteen went to discos there"… "my mum worked there in the 1960s"... "my grandad was working on the roof in the 1950s, lost his footing and fell off. He landed on a pile of sand, got up and walked to Lloyd's Hospital – broken arm, scratches and bruises"… "my friend and I worked there in the 1960s"... "I worked there as a plumber after the fire"… "my dad worked there as a night porter for a few years in the late 1960s. He was very discreet so never told us what he saw"… "I worked for Mr Crocker who owned it in the 1970s"… "my brother worked there as a chef for a time"… "my mum worked there for a while as a waitress"… "I was a commis chef there and I worked there for around eight months when the Crockers owned it"… "my granddad Frank Yates was a chef there in the sixties. My mum can remember going down to the kitchen. There was an Italian waiter working there"… "my aunt managed the front of the hotel and my mother ran the kitchen and the dining room"… "I was the porter there in 1964."

Others remember specific events: "I had my wedding reception there"… "many a happy night there dancing"… "Bridlington Lions used to hold the Carnival Queen Contest there"… "I remember seeing Peter Gordeno the dancer there"… "I used to go to dances there"… "they had ballroom dancing there on a Wednesday night"… "I went to my cousin's twenty-first birthday party there"… "I remember in the early 1950s attending kids' parties there, and I also went back in the 1960s. The local Musicians' Union members organised a dance with the Stanley Ashforth Trio and one or two other dance band trios. I was in a rock band at the time (The Zircons). We turned the volume up and had a great time"… "allegedly mine was the last wedding reception held there in December 1974"… "sad end to a beautiful building – my late sister had her wedding reception there"… "as a girl in my early teens I was a member of the Red Cross. We were invited to baby-sit the children of folk attending a course while they were at a ball on their final night. My friend and I had to go between floors to check on several children. The lift broke down and we were stuck for several hours. Happily the babies were all ok!"… "I had my first wedding reception there"…"I used to attend what was called the 'League of Pity' parties. I think it was the junior part of the NSPCC. We collected money in blue eggs and we received blue-bird badges. It seemed an enormous ballroom to a small child in the 1950s"... "I played in the dance hall with our band 'The Boltones' in the 1960s"... "we had a lot of fun playing there"... "I used to go there for the Coss Bone Fertilizer Christmas children's parties. They were fantastic and we all got a present from Father Christmas plus a lucky bag including sixpence. Super memories from the '50s"... "I had my twenty-first birthday party there and my mates gave me twenty-one bumps, threw me in the air for the last one and let me crash to the parquet floor in the ballroom!"... "the first time I ever went there was as a six-year-old attending the RAF Driffield kids Christmas party in 1956. Hokey Cokey and other dances in the ballroom. Sandwiches, iced buns and jelly, and then into a darkened side room for cartoons on a stand-up screen. Sent home with a brown paper bag of oranges, apples and nuts"..."I remember the discos – Bachman Turner Overdrive ('You ain't seen nothing yet')"... "The Territorials used to hold their children's parties there around the 1950s"... "I used to perform on the grass in the Bridlington Majorettes"... "I once did a disco there when I was working for a local DJ"... "my grandfather used to drink there most nights in the 1960s"... "we had our engagement party there in 1974. The in-drink was lager and blackcurrant"... "I played at a number of dances and parties there in the 1950s with Eddie Harper and Stan Ashforth bands and others"... "Billie Crompton resurrected it as a sort of nightclub where we used to go and watch acts perform like the Barron Knights"... "I remember Margaret Thatcher being on the front lawn for a ceremony of sorts"... "I once saw Matt Monro there"... "We used to have our Christmas dinner there. I loved getting dressed up in our Christmas outfits, knowing what a wonderful meal we would get. The atmosphere was all celebration and joy."

Some can recall the freedom of those carefree days: "we used to get up to all sorts of fun in the many cellar rooms, and play cricket on the front lawn with the children of the owners. Shame it's gone. It was a splendid place"… "my dad used to deliver fruit and vegetables. The cellar was like the catacombs and I remember the dumb-waiter. I used to love playing with it."… "I remember that cellar – quite spooky"… "you could get lost in all those rooms in the basement"… "I used to play football on the lawns before the Punch and Judy Shows, and after that it was down to the Cut and swim out to the rafts"… "occasionally we used to run through the rotating front door and out again on the way back to the Red House 1964-66"… "I remember roller-skating up and down the corridors"… "we used to stop the lift at a floor, press the alarm buttons and run!"… "one year while staying there my friend and I put blue dye in the newly built pond in the adjacent Beaconsfield Gardens. The Mayor came to open it and got a bit of a shock!"… "what happened under the bridge stayed under the bridge!"

One member of the staff clearly made a very strong impression on guests: "had a wonderful cocktail barman in the 1950s called Johnny"… "we got a lovely cocktail here … a man called Johnny"… "I remember Johnny's cocktail bar drinking Blue Horizons"… "I worked there one summer in 1960 as an assistant barman to Johnny in the cocktail bar and got about two shillings and sixpence an hour"… "Johnny, the chirpy cocktail waiter who served Blue Horizon cocktails, won a number of cocktail competitions for five years running"… "my granddad was Johnny Smith who worked behind the bar with my grandma"... "I still have a photo of Johnny the cocktail waiter on my bedroom wall!"... "Johnny the cocktail waiter used to make the children a non-alcoholic cocktail he called 'Jungle Juice' to make them feel grown-up."

Some mention particular aspects of the design of the hotel: 'it looked so different in the 1960s with the columns at the front painted to resemble marble"... "I thought it was really posh when I was small"... "it had a lovely sprung dance floor".

There was always a sense of mystery about the fires in the 1970s: "I was told a guy fell asleep with a lit cigarette – I think he was the one who died but I can't be sure"... "I recall him being a chef at the hotel, smoking in bed"... "I worked with the man who died in the fire. It was one of the waiters. He started it and he died in it"... "a neighbour was a fireman and he went to it".

Some tales are best left anonymous: "a friend worked at The Alex in the 1960s, and had a girlfriend on the staff. All the staff lived on the top floor, men at one end and women at the other, separated by a locked door outside the Matron's Room. Neither were ever allowed into the other's quarters. One night, my friend climbed out of his bedroom window and across the roof. He entered his girlfriend's window and spent the night there. On the way back he slipped and fell, grabbed a gutter and hung there in a state of utter panic. Eventually he managed to scramble back onto the roof and got back into his own room. He sat on the bed shaking like a leaf and vowed never to attempt it again!"

It is fitting the last two of the Facebook contributions are more personal:

The first is a "what might have been": "my parents were going to buy this place and I used to enjoy it and run around all the rooms when it was empty and partly derelict. We had great fun! The deal never came off and it was demolished."

The second is loveliest and kept to last: "my grandparents had their first date in that hotel, and then my grandma worked in the tea room on the front lawns."

When reading through those wonderful memories, it does seem, in a few cases, that discretion is the better part of valour and a thinly veiled anonymity is the best way to protect the guilty!

One or two contributors, however, have kindly agreed to be named alongside their more detailed recollections.

Judy Wilson offered some very personal memories: "My sisters and I remember going to the hospital balls at The Alex in the 1940s and 1950s when we were young. The first part of the evening was for young children and was fancy dress. I was a gypsy and my youngest sister remembers being a rosebud in pink satin. Later in the evening the little ones went home, and the teenagers and adults continued with the ball. We felt very grown up. A friend of mine tells me that the Round Table and Ladies Circle used to hold their meetings at the hotel, and they put on entertainments, one of which was the Black and White Minstrel Show.

"My husband and I had our wedding reception there in October 1960 as it was considered the place to be. It was actually a rather faded, draughty place, and any hot food was carried through from the kitchens at the back of the hotel, so was cooling rapidly by the time the guests received it. I can remember going away and feeling very elegant in a new red coat, standing at the top of the steps and saying goodbye to everyone."

John Walker remembers one special evening with nostalgia and gratitude: "I remember in 1974 or 1975 the banquet and dance that SATRA Motors held for their staff, who were from all nationalities. Based in Carnaby conveniently near the ports of the Humber, SATRA Motors (Soviet American Trading and Retail Association) was a gigantic international firm headed up by two Russian Armenians, Challekian and Ostomeld. This company imported Moskvich and Lada cars and Cossack motorbikes in huge numbers, and they really did share the profits with the workers at Christmas, giving enormous bonuses (sometimes of several thousands). All the ladies were given Ciro pearls, and the families were presented with the biggest hampers you ever saw!"

From Billy Lester came a record of both the highs and the lows (literally!) of life at The Alex: "It was a beautiful building and I was lucky enough to have spent my late teens and early twenties attending mostly Saturday night dances there when they used to have a mix of 'known dance groups' and also local beat groups performing there. I was a member of a local beat group called 'The Electrons' which later became 'The Corvettes' and we used to get booked for Saturday night gigs there around the early to mid-sixties. I remember that there was always a great atmosphere in the ballroom and it was a popular venue for locals wanting to meet up for a drink or two and maybe take to the dance floor for rock and roll with the girls.

"I also remember one guitarist in our beat group was a painter and decorator in his main employment and was employed to help paint the outside of the Alexandra. As you can imagine, it was a big job, taking weeks to decorate with only ladders as there was no scaffolding. It was during this time that he got a bit complacent, and whilst he was painting on a corner of the building, he reached over a bit too far and the wind and his weight caused the ladder to topple resulting in him falling down from nearly the top and landing on the ground. He broke several bones in his body including his back. Needless to say he was out of action, both with his brush and his guitar, for quite a long time, but very lucky to be still alive."

Most but not all of those memories arose from one source, the Facebook Group "Bridlington The Good Old Days" created by Helen Blackburn. Nearly all are astonishingly warm, celebrating times of coming together for fun and good company. Why is this so remarkable? In a strange way, memories of an old and vanished hotel, coming through a very modern means of communicating, just underlines something that has been so important for all human beings since the dawn of civilisation right through to today – the absolute importance of good company.

Once again, we are drawn back to that picture of one of the original shareholders, R. N. Beauvais, a long serving churchwarden at the Priory Church listening each week to the familiar stories of the Bible. From the opening pages of the Book of Genesis, he would have heard the spiritual story of creation designed to answer the question: Why are we here? Today, whether or not we regard it as a true story, it is most certainly a story with a truth. It says that when God made everything He declared at the end of each day as He made the sky, the land, the trees and plants, the animals and so on: "It is good." Then finally He made Adam, and at this point He said "It is not good: it is not good that you should be alone." Consequently, he made Eve for companionship. Whatever our spiritual beliefs, it is an early story underlining the common wisdom that we are made not for lonely isolation but for companionship, good company, togetherness. In its time, The Alex most certainly played an important part in forging good relationships and happy memories. At a time when isolation and loneliness seem to be twin scourges of modern society, this has to be, surely, a very positive cause for gratitude and celebration.

28. THE SPIRIT OF THE ALEX LIVES ON!

The Alexandra Hotel was born in the nineteenth century at a time of great optimism and adventure. Daring entrepreneurs caught the mood of the age, and invested money, time and imagination. The hotel had been conceived and was given birth by those with a sense of both the present and the future. They realised Bridlington was ready for new confidence as a seaside resort.

Like all creations, the hotel itself lived through its challenging infancy, exciting adolescence, gentle maturity, gradual decline, and eventual inevitable demise. After the fires, the building stood boarded up and empty before being demolished in 1976. Abandoned, it was a discouraging eyesore on the seafront, and plans for a more modest hotel on the site never materialised.

Walking past, all sorts of emotions came to the fore in people's minds and hearts – sadness, anger, anxiety, depression – and then gradually as the bereavement process settled, acceptance gave way to talk of possibilities for the site.

Eventually, on the site where once people came to stay for a while to enjoy the salt air and the huge seascapes, in 1986 Tay Buildings constructed a complex of new apartments in which people could live throughout the whole year. In its brochure for the apartments, Tay Homes prided itself on "designing and building new homes of character and individuality...proudly bringing a rather special blend of design philosophy to Bridlington." It boasted, "an interesting blend of homes perfectly in tune with its surroundings and with those subtle touches of design flair which make it so different." It continued that this new development was "...in an enviable seafront position just off the promenade. Offering breathtaking views south over the harbour and north to Flamborough Head, it would be hard to find a more desirable setting... Care is taken to individualise the appearance of each new development undertaken, something Tay Homes considers important in these days of mass production." Somehow, it seems these words written in the 1980s could just as well have been proudly written by the architect and builders of the Alexandra Hotel in the 1860s.

Sixty-five apartments on three and four floors were built in four phases, each being sold in stages to part-fund the costs of the next phase. In 1986 new life in the shape of the aptly-named Alexandra Court was emerging on the site, made possible by new entrepreneurs able, once again, to catch the mood of the age and act with determination and vision.

Even today, the memory of that wonderful lady, Princess Alexandra, is being kept alive as the new apartments were called Alexandra Court, accessed from Alexandra Drive. The Alexandra Complex of holiday apartments sits in Alexandra Drive itself. The right of way along the seafront between the front lawn and the beach is still called Alexandra Promenade, and just to the south there are still the small Alexandra Gardens. On the northern boundary of the site is Alexandra Walk, allowing pedestrians to walk from Flamborough Road to the Alexandra Promenade. From 1989 until 1994 the Alexandra Bowling Club, now with its own green on South Marine Drive, originally met on what had been the hotel's front lawn, but still bears the same name.

And who knows what else locally has been named after her over the years? For example, in the 1860s there was the Bridlington Alexandra Brass Band, led by its conductor, Mr T Macken. Were these musicians based at the hotel? Did they play in the ballroom, on the front lawns or even on the beach? Or were they simply a local group of musicians adopting the name? For how many years did they play together? Like so much it all remains a mystery, but whatever the answers, the adoption of the name seems very fitting. It conjures up a picture of people enjoying themselves by the seaside and returning home feeling better.

In her day, Princess Alexandra stood elegant, loyal and patient, serving her people faithfully, through all the traumas and challenges of her life. In Bridlington today, her legacy remains in the town through all the places bearing her name around the site of the old hotel.

From the last quarter of the twentieth century onwards, further afield in the town other new ventures also were stirring. North Promenade was renewed celebrating its spaciousness with a variety of pavement designs, wall sculptures, arches, colonnades and seating along its way. South Promenade was redesigned and updated with flair and practicality in mind. The Spa Theatre complex on South Beach was transformed at a cost of over twenty million pounds to offer world class facilities. A new Leisure Centre, which cost nearly as much, boasting swimming pools, a fitness centre and a variety of other facilities, rose on North Beach encouraging a new pride in the town. Nearby Sewerby Hall was renewed with grants of over two million pounds. A new Lifeboat Station has been built to match the sweeping architecture of the nearby Spa. Two new modern hotels have been built with more to come. The town centre is the subject of ongoing regeneration, offering green space, a pleasant walkway beside the Gipsey Race, and new shops. Dreams about a small marina to complement the harbour keep reappearing.

These are all about a town finding a new sense of purpose as older industries fade, tastes change and previous ways disappear, but new sources of money arise, and new possibilities dawn. To this day, Bridlington's double-act of being both a working harbour and a holiday resort sit together very comfortably: work and pleasure each add to the special interest and colourful life of the town.

Above all, Bridlington is a town of generous hospitality. For those at sea, the harbour has always offered a welcome and encouraged passing ships to take shelter from the storms of the North Sea in Bridlington Bay, known as the "Bay of Refuge". Here, seafarers could stay awhile, recuperate, mend themselves and their ships, and leave with renewed vigour. Similarly, on the land, for centuries Bridlington Priory had been hospitable to pilgrims coming to visit the shrine of St John of Bridlington with the same aim in mind.

Further afield, all over the country Princess Alexandra has had countless numbers of hospitals very appropriately dedicated to her name – hospitals offering hospitality as people are cured and healed for a new adventure in life. Nurses in the Queen Alexandra Royal Nursing Corps carry her name as they tend wounded members of the armed forces to this day.

In its day, the Alexandra Hotel stood firmly in this tradition of hospitality, and today in Bridlington and beyond the spirit of The Alex most certainly lives on with a generous and welcoming smile.

The Garden Café on the front lawn by Trinity Cut, with the hotel's nine-hole mini golf course behind

In the Second World War a gun-emplacement was built at the foot of the steps of Alexandra Walk leading down to the promenade. The hotel is in the top left corner.

The shock from the blast of a nearby parachute land mine in the Second World War shattered all the hotel's rear windows, demolished the outhouses and damaged the roof.

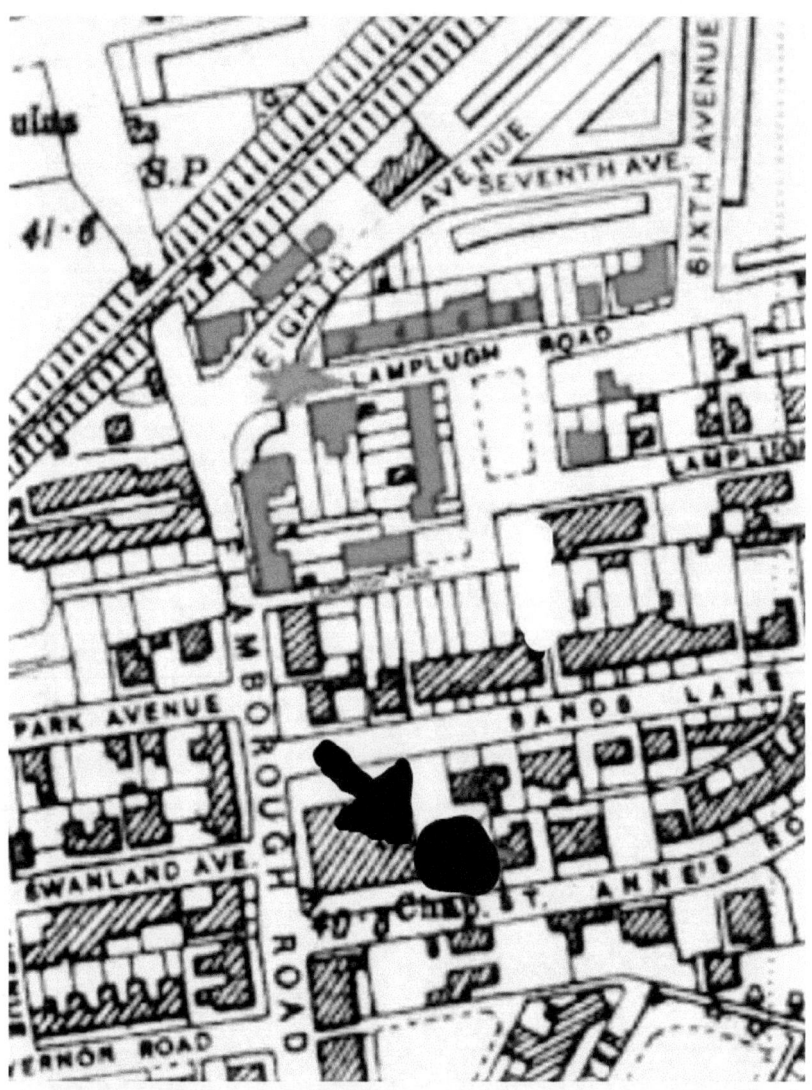

A map of wartime damage in Bridlington shows where a parachute land mine hit St Anne's Convalescent Home in 1941, just 100 yards to the north of The Alex – the probable cause of the hotel's bomb damage.

The decorated pillars, with carpets and wallpaper of sumptuous red and gold, invited guests in the 1960s to enjoy a very comfortable holiday.

The ballroom with its mirrored pillars in the 1960s.

The dining room of the 1960s, complete with immaculate table cloths, and red, gold and white décor.

The 1960s cocktail bar.

Johnny Smith the cocktail waiter with his wife Sadie, who are so fondly remembered by many guests. Note Johnny's shirt embroidered with the monogram "A H" each side for "Alexandra Hotel".

Alexandra Hotel

BRIDLINGTON'S LEADING HOTEL
CAR PARK - PRIVATE GROUNDS - FACING SEA
CENTRAL HEATING - LIFT TO ALL FLOORS
75 BEDROOMS WITH H. & C. WATER

SMOKE ROOM AND COCKTAIL BARS
. . . BALLROOM . . .
ALL AMENITIES FOR CONFERENCES

Tel.: 2254

An advertisement boasting 75 bedrooms and a "smoke room" as a special attraction.

ALEXANDRA HOTEL
BRIDLINGTON

Telephone Reception 2254　　　　　　　　Visitors 2045

RESTAURANTS, BARS, BALLROOM OPEN TO NON-RESIDENT

Dancing every evening during the season

★

75 Bedrooms with H. & C.　　　　　Central Heating
Lift to all Floors　　　　　　　　　　　Restaurant
Ballroom　　　　Cocktail Lounge　　Lounge Bar etc.

★

Luncheons, Afternoon Teas, Dinners, served daily including Sunday
Ideal position overlooking the Sea
Large private Lawns leading onto the Beach

An advertisement noting 75 bedrooms "all with hot and cold"
as a welcome feature!

An advertisement featuring the fact that some bedrooms have a private bathroom and it is under the ownership of Mr & Mrs N G Crocker.

Alexandra Hotel

BRIDLINGTON.

Telephone: No. 2254.

Telegrams: "Bridlington 2254"

NOTICES TO VISITORS.

Visitors are requested to Register their Names upon arrival, thereby obviating any delay in the delivery of Letters, Telegrams, etc.

The Proprietors will not be responsible for any Property lost in the Hotel, unless deposited with the Management for Security, and a Receipt taken for same.
(Vide Act of Parliament, 26 & 27 Vict. Cap. 41, Sec. 1) a copy of which is exhibited in the Hall of this Hotel, as required by the Act.

TABLE d'HOTE MEALS
are served at the following Hours :—
BREAKFAST from 8.0 a.m. to 9.30 a.m.
LUNCHEON „ 1.0 p.m. to 2.0 p.m.
DINNER „ 7.0 p.m. to 8.0 p.m.
(Afternoon Tea served in Lounge from 4 p.m.)

An extra charge is made for all meals served in Bedrooms and Private Rooms
All Accounts are presented for payment Weekly.
A 10% Service charge will be added to the Bill in lieu of gratuities to Staff.

Cheques cannot be cashed unless 4 days' notice is given for clearance.

Departures :—Visitors are requested to give Notice of same at the Office, a Day beforehand if possible, but not later than 12 noon on the Day of their departure.
THIS HOTEL IS FULLY LICENSED.
Visitors providing their own Wines, &c. will be charged corkage.
Chambermaids are on duty until 8.30 p.m.
Banquets, Receptions, Conferences, etc. Catered for.
This Hotel is appointed A.A. — R.A.C.
No responsibility is accepted for Cars, or other vehicles parked outside or near this Hotel.

These HOTEL "TARIFF-FRAMES" and "THE HANDY" Guide are published by
THE HOTEL & GENERAL ADVERTISING COMPANY, LIMITED,
TEMPLE HOUSE, TEMPLE AVENUE, LONDON, E.C.4.

VISITORS are respectfully informed that the TRADE ANNOUNCEMENTS appearing on either side of the "Tariff-Frame" are inserted with the approval of the Manager of the Hotel, and may therefore be patronised with safety and satisfaction.

HOTELS RECOMMENDED
These Hotels have been inspected by us and are in every way thoroughly reliable.

BOURNEMOUTH		Imperial
CROMER		Hotel de Paris
DARLINGTON		King's Head
DUNDEE		Royal British
KESWICK		Armathwaite Hall
MORECAMBE		Elms
NORTH BERWICK		Imperial
ULVERSTON		Sun
WINDERMERE		Crown
WORKSOP		Lion

For a complete list of RELIABLE HOTELS with full particulars Local Notes, Maps, etc., see
"THE HANDY" GUIDE
Gratis upon application at this and all other first-class Hotels.

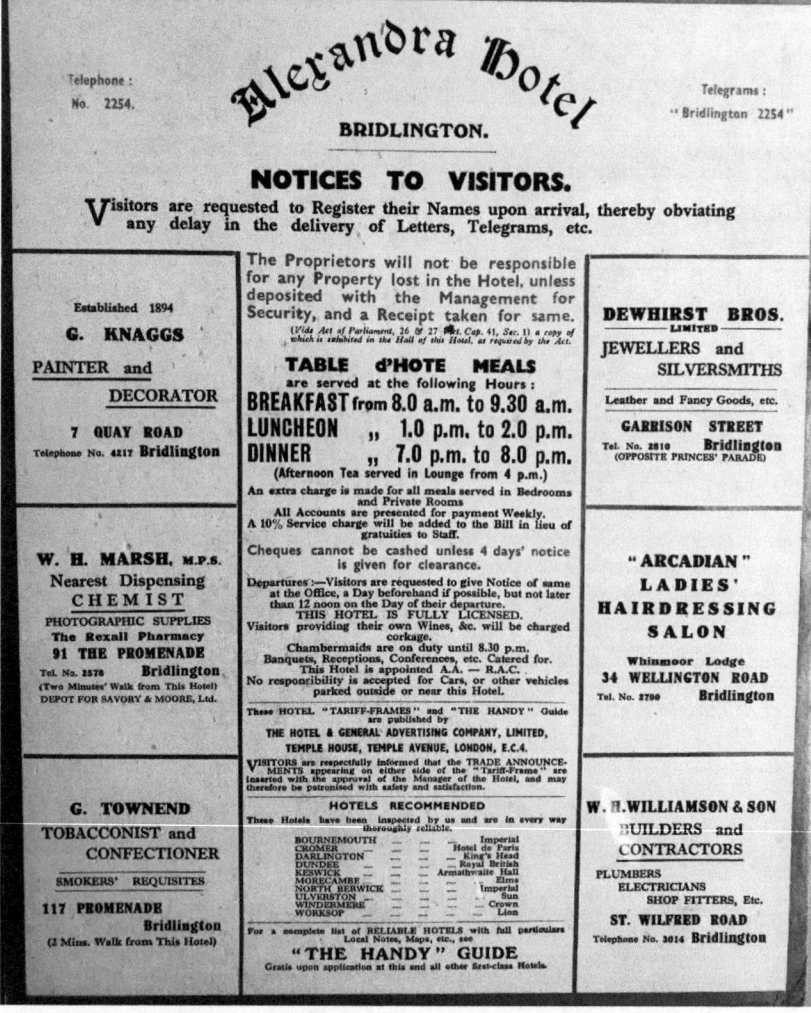

Established 1894
G. KNAGGS
PAINTER and DECORATOR
7 QUAY ROAD
Telephone No. 4217 Bridlington

W. H. MARSH, M.P.S.
Nearest Dispensing
CHEMIST
PHOTOGRAPHIC SUPPLIES
The Rexall Pharmacy
91 THE PROMENADE
Tel. No. 2576 Bridlington
(Two Minutes' Walk from This Hotel)
DEPOT FOR SAVORY & MOORE, Ltd.

G. TOWNEND
TOBACCONIST and CONFECTIONER
SMOKERS' REQUISITES
117 PROMENADE
Bridlington
(2 Mins. Walk from This Hotel)

DEWHIRST BROS.
LIMITED
JEWELLERS and SILVERSMITHS
Leather and Fancy Goods, etc.
GARRISON STREET
Tel. No. 2810 Bridlington
(OPPOSITE PRINCES' PARADE)

"ARCADIAN"
LADIES'
HAIRDRESSING
SALON
Whinmoor Lodge
34 WELLINGTON ROAD
Tel. No. 2790 Bridlington

W. H. WILLIAMSON & SON
BUILDERS and CONTRACTORS
PLUMBERS
ELECTRICIANS
SHOP FITTERS, Etc.
ST. WILFRED ROAD
Telephone No. 3014 Bridlington

Inside each bedroom in the 1960s was a notice giving information about the rules of the hotel and the times of meals.

William and Isabella Hatje, whose family owned the hotel from the 1930s until 1964.

In 1955 Walter Hatje married Kathleen Robinson, photographed here on the steps of the hotel. From left to right: Olive Robinson (sister of the bride, teacher at Moorfield School), Valerie Hatje (wife of Norman Hatje), Norman Hatje (older brother of the groom), William Hatje (eldest brother of the groom), Walter Hatje (groom), Stuart Downs (husband of Lily, nee Hatje), Kathleen (Kay) Robinson (bride), George Armitage Robinson (father of the bride), Vaila Frankland (nee Hatje, sister of the groom), Isabella Gordon Hatje (mother of the groom), Eric Killingley (brother in law of the bride), Joyce Killingley (nee Robinson, sister of the bride), Lily Downs (nee Hatje, sister of the groom), and in the front the two children: Leonor Frankland (niece of the groom) and Susan Killingley (niece of the bride).

The headstone marking the grave in Bridlington cemetery of
William Hatje and Isabella Gordon Hatje.

A brain-teaser: do you recognise any of the people at this event in the hotel's gardens? Might it be a Ladies' Lifeboat Guild Garden Party? From the ladies' dresses and the cars in the background could it be in the 1950s? Or do you have other ideas?

A later and more imaginative advertisement for the hotel.

Engrossed in reading and knitting, who were these two ladies?

Alice and Stanley Tiffany owned the hotel in the mid-1960s.

Alice and Stanley Tiffany's three daughters, with their husbands, who all ran the hotel – Les and Janice, Jerry and Ann, Pauline and Jim.

Cover page of 1965 Christmas holiday package brochure.

PROGRAMME

FRIDAY, DECEMBER 24th. CHRISTMAS EVE

6.30 p.m. – 7.00 p.m.	Welcome to the Alexandra Hotel Sherry Party. Guests are invited to take Sherry with the Directors in the Ballroom.
7.00 p.m.	Christmas Eve Dinner.
9.15 p.m. – 11.45 p.m.	Grand Christmas Dance.
11.45 p.m.	Carols with the Geoffrey Heald-Smith Choristers.

TELEVISION

SATURDAY, DECEMBER 25th. CHRISTMAS DAY

8.00 a.m. – 9.30 a.m.	Breakfast. Details of Church Services can be obtained from Reception.
12.00 noon	Luncheon and Childrens Christmas Dinner.
4.00 p.m.	Tea in the Lounges. Guess the weight of the Christmas Cake and win a bottle of Champagne.
2.30 p.m. – 5.00 p.m.	Children's Christmas Party. Santa Claus will be there with gifts for our young guests.
7.00 p.m. – 11.30 p.m.	Traditional Christmas Dinner in the Dining Room with Party Games to follow in the Ballroom.
10.30 p.m. – 11.00 p.m.	Supper Buffet.

TELEVISION.

Page one of the 1965 Christmas holiday package brochure. Note "Sherry with the Directors", rather like "Dining at the Captain's Table" on a cruise ship today?

CHRISTMAS 1965

SUNDAY, DECEMBER 26th

8.00 a.m. – 9.30 a.m.	Breakfast.
10.30 a.m. – 3.00 p.m.	Mystery Tour with Packed Lunches.
4.00 p.m. – 5.30 p.m.	Tea time Technicolour Film Show in the Ballroom.
7.00 p.m.	Dinner.
8.15 p.m. – 11.00 p.m.	Masked Fancy Dress Ball. All Guests are respectfully requested to come prepared to take part in the Fancy Dress Ball.
9.30 p.m.	B.B.C. Singing Star John Lawrenson entertains.

TELEVISION

MONDAY, DECEMBER 27th. BOXING DAY

8.00 a.m. – 9.30 a.m.	Breakfast.
10.00 a.m. – 12.30 p.m.	Coaches leave the Hotel for the meet of the Middleton East Hunt, and Coffee at Driffield.
1.30 p.m.	Late Luncheon.
4.00 p.m.	Tea in the Lounge.
7.00 p.m.	Dinner.
8.30 p.m. – 12.30 a.m.	Grand Ball and Cabaret.

TELEVISION

TUESDAY, DECEMBER 28th

8.00 a.m. – 9.30 a.m.	Breakfast.
12.00 noon	Luncheon.

TARIFF

For any period up to 4 days — 26 to 28 guineas per person inclusive.
Children sharing parents room:

Up to 2 years of age — 4 guineas.
2 — 10 years of age — 21 guineas.

A 10% Service Charge will be added to All Accounts.

Page two of the 1965 Christmas holiday package brochure which includes "Technicolour Film Show", "Masked Fancy Dress Ball" and excursion to watch The Middleton East Hunt.

72 Bedrooms

Good Food and Service

Fully Licensed Lounge and Cocktail Bars

Spacious Lounges

Television Room

Lift to all floors

H. & C. Power and Shaving Points in all rooms

Central Heating

Special parking facilities at the front of the Hotel

Childrens suppers are served in the bedrooms

Night Porter

Dogs: In view of many unfortunate experiences in the past we regret that dogs are not allowed

Open all the year

The 1966 brochure with the carefully worded: "Dogs: In view of many unfortunate experiences in the past we regret that dogs are not allowed." We can only guess…! Note also the seagull at the bottom –love them or hate them, even then seagulls were a talking point!

ALEXANDRA HOTEL
BRIDLINGTON

wish you a

Very Happy Christmas

1966

Cover of the 1966 Christmas holiday package brochure.

World class group, The Rolling Stones, stayed at The Alex in the mid-sixties, indicating the status of Bridlington as a resort and the high calibre of the hotel.

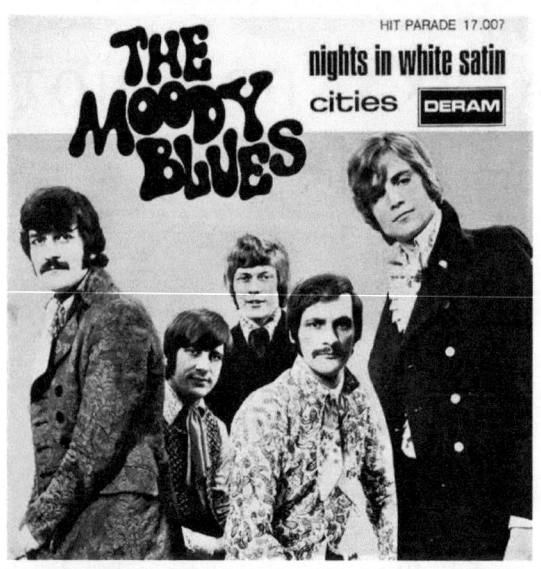

The Birmingham–based group The Moody Blues, who regularly topped the charts, stayed at the hotel in the sixties.

Still touring today, The Hollies stayed at The Alex in the sixties when their albums were outselling most others.

Part of the "Liverpool Sound", The Swinging Blue Jeans were guests at the hotel in the sixties.

Britain's best-loved comedy duo, Morecambe and Wise, enjoyed relaxing in the company of the owners, the Tiffany family, while staying at The Alex when they topped the bill at The Spa.

A year before it closed, an advertisement from the 1975 Town Guide features a very busy season of entertainment with Music Hall Revues six days a week.

Fire engines attend the blaze in 1975.

A less-edifying view of the rear of the hotel towards the end of its days.

The hotel finally closes its doors in 1976.

Demolition in 1976.

Demolition of the hotel in progress.

The demolition is nearly complete.

Brochure for the new Alexandra Court apartments built on the site by Tay Homes.

In 1986 construction begins on the new Alexandra Court apartments.

Alexandra Court apartments now stand on the site of the hotel.

The Alex had its own crested crockery. The hotel was advertised in 1872 as "Taylor's Alexandra Hotel." In 1866 Edwin Taylor was the first owner. His name is on the Census of 1871 but not of 1881. The crockery is therefore a souvenir of the very early days.

Mementos from the past: a group of some of the hotel's crested table ware. The white crockery had deep red and blue decoration.

A hotel crested plate.

A hotel crested sugar bowl.

A hotel crested silver salt cellar.

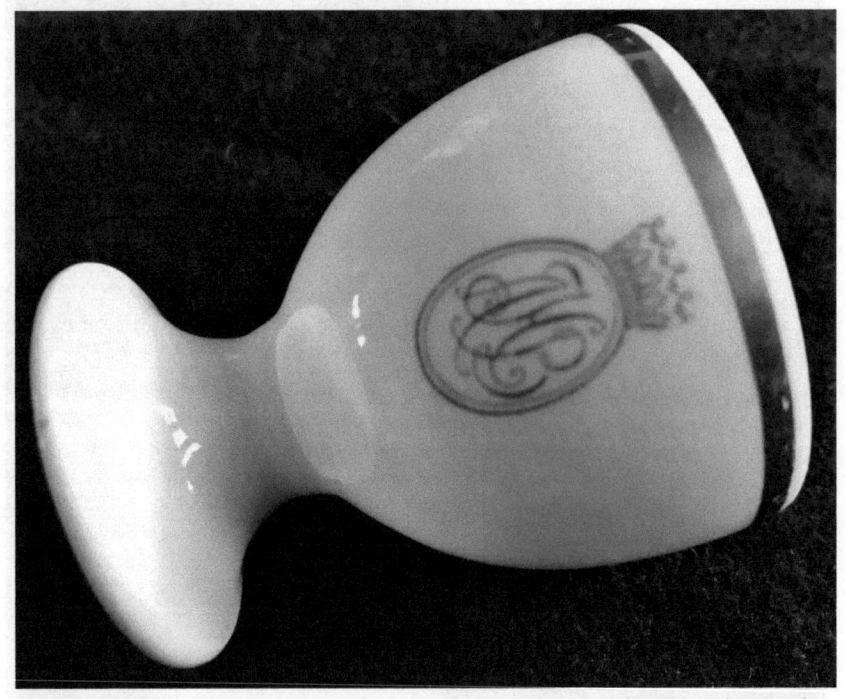

A hotel white china egg cup with the gold monogram "AHB" – Alexandra Hotel Bridlington.

A rubber ink stamp for marking papers with the words "Alexandra Hotel Bridlington".

An embossed teaspoon and fork stamped "The Alexandra Hotel". Does anyone know why the prongs of the fork are of different lengths mirroring the fingers of a human hand?

The handle of a silver-plated fork with the wording "Alexandra Hydro Hotel". This must date it between 1906 and 1911 when The Alex was marketed as a hydro-hotel. The fork was manufactured by James Deakin and Sons Ltd of Sheffield, renowned for very high class cutlery.

The handle of an undated silver plated teaspoon with the wording "Alexandra Hotel Bridlington".

The steps down to the promenade are all that physically now remain of the original hotel building.

The hotel may have disappeared, but the stories about the people continued. Charles Harry Dowson worked as a waiter at The Alex in 1937, aged 19. During the Second World War he served in the Royal Canadian Air Force as a mechanic, and then worked for General Electrics, Canada. After retiring he flew a Cessna 150 aircraft solo, enjoyed snow-shoeing and cross country skiing. Quite a waiter!"

BIBLIOGRAPHY

Janice Anderson, Edmund Swinglehurst: The Victorian and Edwardian Seaside. Pub: Country Life Books (1978)

Gertrude Attwood: The Wilsons of Tranby Croft. Pub: Hutton Press (1988)

Karen Averbury: Britain's Heritage – Seaside Hotels. Pub: Amberley (2018)

Malcolm Barker: The Golden Age of the Yorkshire Seaside. Pub: Great Northern Books (2002)

Bayle Museum Trust: Bridlington Memories. Pub: The Bayle Museum Trust (1995)

British Library: The British Newspaper Archive.

Tom Brown: Bridlington In Old Picture Postcards. Pub: European Library (1987)

Kenneth Elsom: Postcards of Bridlington. Pub: The Avenues Press (1991)

Lara Feigel and Alexandra Harris: Modernism on Sea: Art and Culture at the British Seaside. Pub: Peter Lang Ltd (2011)

Ron Freethy: Yorkshire on Holiday. Pub: Dalesman (2013)

Fred Grey: Designing the Seaside. Pub: Reaction Books (2006)

Stuart Hylton: The British Seaside: An Illustrated History. Pub: Amberley Publishing (2018)

Kenneth Lindley: Seaside Architecture. Pub: Hugh Evelyn Ltd (1973)

John Hannavy: The English Seaside in Victorian and Edwardian Times. Pub: Shire Publications (2003)

John Heywood: Beside The Seaside. Pub: Pen and Sword Ltd (2017)

Mike Hitches: Bridlington Through Time. Pub: Amberley Publishing (2012)

David & Susan Neave: Bridlington – An introduction to its history and buildings. Pub: Smith Settle (2000)

David Neave: Port, Resort and Market Town: A History of Bridlington. Pub: Hull Academic Press ((2000)

Jonathan Oates: John George Haigh – The Acid Bath Murderer. Pub: Pen & Sword (2014)

Karen Snowden: Bathing Costumes. (Article available at Whitby Museum)

Ian & Margaret Sumner: Bridlington – Britain in old photographs. Pub: Budding Books (1995)

Patricia Susan, Dixon MacArthur: Not a Guide to Bridlington. Pub: The History Press (2013)

Derek Taylor, David Bush: The Golden Age of British Hotels. Pub: Northwood Publication (1974)

Fred Walkington MBE: The Bridlington Lifeboat. Pub: Phillimore & Co. (2005)

John K. Walton: The British Seaside: Holidays and Resorts in the Twentieth Century. Pub: Manchester University Press (2000)

Fiona Watson: Bygone Bridlington. Pub: English Heritage (date unstated)

Alan Whitworth: Aspects of the Yorkshire Coast. Pub: Wharncliffe Books (2000)

Peter Williams: The English Seaside. Pub: English Heritage (2005)

Mike Wilson: A Postcard From Bridlington. Pub: Prestyme House (1986)

Mike Wilson: My Bridlington. Pub: Free Spirit Writers (2008)

Mike Wilson: We're Back in Brid. Pub: Free Spirit Writers (2016)

Robert Woodhouse: East Yorkshire Curiosities. Pub: The History Press (2010)

Michael Wray: Bridlington in Old Postcards. Pub: East Coast Books (2006)

ACKNOWLEDGEMENTS

The staffs of the following resource centres have all been wonderfully helpful and so encouraging in the development of this story:

The Bayle Museum, Bridlington.
Bridlington Local Studies Library, Bridlington Library.
East Riding Archives and Local Studies, Treasure House, Beverley.
The Hull History Centre, Hull.

A huge number of individual people have been amazingly supportive and informative along the way.

- ➢ Members of the Bridlington Augustinian Society, especially John Walker and Rick Hudson for painstakingly reading the text and offering corrections, additions and anecdotes.

- ➢ Dr David Neave for background material about Mr Percy Newbound.

- ➢ Sarah Davidson for providing so much detail about her family, the Hatjes, who owned the hotel for thirty years, and for permission to use her photographs of family members, hotel crockery, Johnny the Cocktail waiter and the bedroom door notice.

- ➢ Janice and Les Hornby with their daughter Amanda for all the information about the years when the Tiffany family owned the hotel, and permission to use photographs of family members and hotel brochures.

➢ Fred Walkington MBE for information about lifeboat launches from Trinity Cut.

➢ For permission to use personal photographs: By courtesy of Andy Day (hotel rubber stamp), Colin Hinson (William and Isabella Hatje's gravestone), Mike Barnard (Adam Faith), Vince Hall (hotel sugar bowl) and Stewart Would (waiter Charles Harry Dowson).

➢ Andy Jefferson for alerting me to so many rarely seen photographs.

➢ For their personal stories: Terrie Britt, Kevin Geraghty, Billy Lester, Rod Lewis, Steve Pepper, Ray Purdy and Judy Wilson.

➢ Lance Cook, John Mosley, Michael Pease, Graham Pilling and Mike Wilson for offering various documents, brochures, local connections and stories.

➢ Contributors to the Facebook Group "Bridlington The Good Old Days", founded by Helen Blackburn, who shared so many memories when an appeal was made:

Jean Artley, Fiona Atacks, Jayne Atkinson, Steven Bean, Mike Barnard, John Billingham, Sidney Bolton, Simon Boulton, Maggie Broom, David Brown, Jill Brown, Dave Causer, Mandy Clay, Lauren Cockerill, Jacqui Copsey, Sarah Davidson, Diane Davison, Margaret Dobson, Janet Dunners Dunwell, Pauline Ellis, Terry Ellis, Geoff Eyre, Jane Farr, Martin Frankish, Jane Gunter, Julie Guy, Juliette Hall, Andrina Hardcastle, June Henry, Stuart Henshall, Susan

Herdsman, Pauline Hick, Andy Hirst, Gordon Holgate, Graham Holgate, Paul Jefferson, Malcolm Jennison, Sue Johnston, Derrick Milson, Gordon Morrice, Sue Murray, Audrey O'Farrell, Robert Michael O'Neill, Janet Parks, Steve Pepper, Ian Phillips, Michael Rice, Pete Robinson, Graham (Rollo) Rollinson, Jackie Sanderson, Richard Sanderson, Paula Searle, Cyril Skinner, Jayne Sissons, Carol Smalley, Tim Smith, Stan Stallard, Lee Stanyard, Jenny Steels, Alan Sunley, Tom Smith, Kevin Tate, Dave Totty, Dominick Umgawa Taylor, Keith Wagstaff, Linda Walkington, Gwyneth Williamson, John Wilson, Jacqui Wright, Anita Wright.

- Jeniffer Williams, who somehow managed to turn my indecipherable scrawl into a typed manuscript, a task few could have achieved, and certainly not with such a willing, uncomplaining and cheerful disposition.

- Susan Hutchinson of Lodge Books, Bridlington, who throughout the process of producing this book has been wonderfully imaginative, efficient and helpful.

- My wife, Diana, who has patiently lived with me while this book has slowly taken shape, and then proof-read the script so carefully.

Without all these people, trying to explore the story of The Alex would not have been so fascinating or so much fun. Their encouragement and interest has made it both personal and possible. However, the author alone is responsible for any errors or omissions.

Every effort has been made to trace copyright holders and to obtain their permission for the use of copyright material. Apologies are offered for any oversights, and the necessary corrections will be incorporated in any future edition.

Video available on You Tube,

complete with big band music and sound effects.

Simply search for

"THE ALEX BRIDLINGTON."

THE ALEX BRIDLINGTON: 1866-1976

YouTube Video